AMERICAN PROBLEMS
BY
WILLIAM E. BORAH

Wm E. Borah

AMERICAN PROBLEMS

A SELECTION OF SPEECHES AND PROPHECIES BY

WILLIAM E. BORAH

EDITED BY

HORACE GREEN

NEW YORK
DUFFIELD & COMPANY
1924

CONTENTS

PREFACE

There are several reasons why the name of William E. Borah has taken root with the American people. One of them may be summed up in the word "independence." Not the least of them is the confidence, deepening year by year, that Mr. Borah is little affected by the political consequence of his utterance on this or that public question. Yet his viewpoint on a great number of questions—whether or not we agree with him at the time—seems to have become, sooner or later, the viewpoint of a majority of the people. Witness his fight against the Versailles Treaty, the fight against the League of Nations, in which he was a pioneer; his stand for restricted immigration and for the release of political prisoners; his still undecided fight against the soldier bonus; his fight for the limitation of naval armament. Indeed it is generally accepted that Mr. Borah was the originator of the famous Washington Disarmament Conference. In the Senate the galleries are packed and his colleagues on both sides of the aisle listen with professional admiration when Borah takes the floor. Without the Idaho senator's powerful personality and delivery the written word is robbed of much power. The speeches are, for some tastes, too much in the vein of old-fashioned oratory— therefore is the substance often overlooked. Because they are for the most part buried in the Congressional Record and because there is in them much of permanent value, their presentation in book form is undertaken as a worthwhile record of political sentiment.. This is done with the senator's approval.

Within his own party Mr. Borah is an out-standing figure in spite of the fact that he has repeatedly refused to be bound by the organization program. Yet he has never bolted, probably never will bolt, and presumably does not desire, or aspire, to be an active presidential candidate. Right or wrong he is a necessary tonic—a progressive within the party; sometimes a radical, but always within the Consitution.

HORACE GREEN.

AMERICAN PROBLEMS

WILLIAM E. BORAH

I

WHY HAS HAMILTON NO STATUE?

(Address delivered at a meeting of the Hamilton Memorial Society, Washington, D. C., January 11, 1910.)

One must be inexcusably ignorant of his country's history not to know, and blindly partizan not to be willing to admit, that this Government of ours was the work of no single individual. Each carried to the work his own material, but when the task was finished and the impressive edifice stood forth, scarcely a piece in the whole mighty structure appeared in its original form. Out of concession and compromise, of clashing judgments and conflicting views, came the finished fabric which has excited the wonder and challenged the admiration of all the civilized people of the earth.

How fortunate for us that by this process, all was done that was done. The confidence and faith, the doubts and fears of all those men are interwoven into this heritage of ours. I am glad that the advices of those who urged a strong government did not in all their fulness

Eventually, May 16, 1923, the Frazer Statue of Hamilton was erected and unveiled on the Treasury Building steps in Washington.

prevail; I rejoice that the jealous guardians of States' Rights were not permitted to have their way as fully as they felt they ought. I am made glad every time I contemplate the work that both Hamilton and Jefferson lived in those days. I find no gratification in groping among the archives of my country for questionable facts upon which to make invidious comparisons. I know as well as anything can be known, dependent upon history, that each excelled in his own particular way, that each wrought in absolute sincerity, gave to the cause the best that was in him both of heart and brain, and that in the final result there was glory enough for all.

But in his sudden rise from obscurity to power; in the wide range and singular brilliancy of his intellect; in his complete mastery of the great problems of that extraordinary era, Alexander Hamilton stood alone—even the masterful spirit of Washington challenged not his supremacy within his own dominion. Every man of his times, willingly or unwillingly, paid homage to his genius, and feared or followed him in his eager, restless, untiring purpose to realize the vast conceptions of his mighty brain. Among a race of intellectual giants, this orphan boy, without family, wealth, or social prestige, had, when thirty years of age, attained an eminence which in some ways divides the admiration of mankind with the Father of Our Country. From the time we search for his lowly origin in a foreign land until he sinks beneath the adventurer's deadly aim, there is a constant attendance of wonder, a fascinating and inexplicable air of mysterious power, threading his whole career. I challenge history to present another like him.

When seventeen, at the gathering "on the fields," he sounded clear and strong the bugle-note of American independence. When eighteen, he handled the weapons of political controversy like a veteran, and stood a dreaded antagonist in that arena where so many enter and so few succeed. While still a youth he won distinction as an artilleryman at Brooklyn, Harlem, and White Plains, and, finally, with Napoleonic dash, stormed the first redoubts at Yorktown, and passed on and out of the war without a blemish upon his record as a soldier. Drawn close to Washington, passing within the view of that cold and dispassionate leader, he won and held throughout his life this great man's love. To Morris, the financier of the Revolution, he offered most valuable suggestions on finance, and clearly disclosed that already he carried within his teeming mind, the great financial system he was afterwards, as Secretary of the Treasury, to mature. As early as 1781, in a letter to Duane, he sketches with the ease and finish of inspiration, the outlines of this great Government. When the constitutional convention adjourned, with the majority of the people in the different States against the federal charter and powerful leaders opposing it, to Hamilton and his masterful presentation of the cause, more than to anyone else, was due the momentous fact of its adoption. In the New York convention he met Clinton in all his power, fortified by State prejudice and a powerful political machine. Twice he was defeated by a vote of 46 to 19, but returned undaunted and unconquerable, to win at last by the sheer force of that will power that grinds ordinary men to atoms—that intellectual wrath and strength against which ordinary mortals cannot stand. It is not too much to say that there was fought the real battle for constitutional government. And during these brief, crowded years, he also became the first lawyer of his day, and stands until now among the foremost of that great profession. Keen, penetrating, searching, all-encompassing in mind, exalted in purpose, persistent and resistless in energy, patriotic and ambitious, he was the most striking and dramatic figure of all. Washington was wise, self-centered, and self-poised; Adams impetuous, able, and forceful; Jefferson engaging, sagacious, cultured, and humane; but Hamilton was the great creative, constructive, vitalizing force—the one who seemed above all others endowed with the divine power to touch and bring forth anew.

And yet nowhere in this statue-crowded city, nor in the lonesome corridors of yonder Capitol, can be found a fit monument to Alexander Hamilton. Why is it? Washington is there, as he should be, first and foremost. But does anyone know upon whom he relied so firmly and continuously as upon the man who is not there? George Clinton is there, whom Hamilton defeated in his heroic effort to secure the adoption of the Constitution and to make possible our Government. Strange irony in this reward a republic gives her creators. What delays the hour when this Government shall do itself honor by honoring Alexander Hamilton? Is it because he never flattered nor turned aside from the clear vision of his intellect to court popular applause; that there is not to be found in all his writings or speeches a line or phrase to indicate that he ever sought to arouse the passions, or enlist the prejudice, or win by sinister means the applause of the multitude? Out of the integrity of his intellect and the high purpose of his soul, he led them. Is it because by searching the pages of bitter political controversy, and reviving and resuscitating the stale slander of another century men are led to say that while manifestly great, he was not divine? We rear monuments to men, not deities. We honor men not because, perchance, in passing through the fiery furnace some charred marks of the conflict remain, but because they did pass through and drew after them the everlasting happiness of their kind. That "This Man receiveth sinners and eateth with them" was the only thing which appealed to the Pharisee; that He healed the sick, restored to sight the blind, and raised the dead, moved these soulless hypocrites not at all. What a dismal place yonder "Hall of Fame" would be if great men had to be as perfect as the rules and demands of small men would make them.

But let the excuse for this delay be what it may; let not this generation share the disgrace. In these days when national questions are forcing us to their solution, let us honor the man who, more than all others, fought for the great national powers now so essential to the people's happiness and the Government's stability.

II

THE BONUS BILL

(Excerpt from Speech in the United States Senate, July 14, 1921.)

Something has been said about postponing the bill for six months and bringing it back in six months from now and considering it. I would not wish to be harsh with anyone who contemplates voting to send the bill to the committee for six months and bringing it out again, but if anything would be characteristic of pure political expediency in this situation it would be precisely that thing. What will be the difference six months from now, so far as the taxpayer, the business man, the laborer, and other conditions are concerned? What could be more discouraging to revival of business than a mere postponement of such obligation. And until business revives there will be unemployment and hungry people. We ought to have the courage, if we are against the proposition, to say so and to say why, and carry it back to the Legion at home and receive their judgment. If it is against us, very well and good; but there is no use to trifle with the proposition by sending it back to the committee for six months and bringing it out when we will be no better off at that time. I do not agree with the argument that is presented for postponement.

The course which this bill has had is already discreditable to the Congress. It was introduced in the House on the 20th of May, 1920, it was reported on the 21st of May, 1920, and passed the House on the 29th of May, 1920, just about the time that the conventions and primaries were being held. It then came to the Senate and went to the Finance Committee and remained there until four days before the adjournment of the last session. Now it is reported out providing nothing to be paid until the 1st day of July, 1922, about the time elections are coming on again.

The embarrassing feature of the situation is that we seem to think there is a very large block of votes represented by the opposition to delaying the bill. My opinion is the block is not so large as it seems to be, but, large or small, we ought at least to pursue a straightforward, continuous course with reference to dealing with a matter of such supreme importance to the people of the United States. If we can not agree to pay the service man, we can at least be candid and honest with him and preserve our own self-respect, even though we lose his political support.

Mr. President, I do not claim that power which can "look into the seeds of time and say which grain will grow and which will not"— far from it. But the man is blind who does not recognize that the most widespread and threatening aspect in public affairs at this time is the feeling upon the part of the people everywhere that their Governments, either through indifference or incapacity, will not or can not relieve them of the crushing burdens under which they are now bending. The ties which bind peoples to their Governments are snapping everywhere. Should we be surprised that it is so? Men seeking office and in public place daily promise to lift the load the people are carrying, yet in the actual result of things there is no relief. Economy is made the shibboleth of political campaigns, and yet there is no economy. Taxes are to be reduced, and yet taxes increase from year to year with remorseless persistency. Extravagance in public expenditures is denounced by all political parties and all men, and yet each party upon coming into power makes the record of its predecessor look modest and respectable. A war is fought to end war, and before the bloody fields are dry

and before the agony of conflict has yielded to
the soothing effects of time the victors begin
to arm against each other—for there is no one
else against whom to arm. And thus more
burdens, more taxes, more misery. How long
this can continue I do not know, but it would
seem in this tortured and torturing hour that
the human family had about reached its Geth-
semane and that some scheme of redemption
ought to be near at hand.

I am positive of one thing, that we can not
long continue along the course we are now
traveling. We seem to think there is no limit
to the people's capacity to pay, and no point
beyond which they can no longer bear up under their load. But there is a limit to their capacity to pay and there is a limit to their endur-
ance, and when either or both are reached God
alone knows what lies beyond. If this brutal
war had not long since inured us to human misery, even present conditions would not be tolerated. Never before in the history of the
world, not even in the night of the Thirty
Years' War or in the Napoleonic era, have
there been such debts, such taxes, such burdens, material, social, or moral, such weight
upon the masses, such misery among the people. Countless thousands are being born into

the world, cursed at birth with disease and withered in limb because of the burden which Governments lay upon their mothers. Millions more are stunted in mind and starved in body because of the cruel environments amidst which they are reared. Upon every hand, in every land, crowding the cities, at home and abroad, are the maimed and broken and the helpless and those shivering on the brink of a suicide's grave. Men who a few months ago had about them the earnings of a lifetime are financially ruined. Business is discouraged, industries are closed, and the swelling armies of the unemployed bid fair to equal the fighting forces of a few months ago. Yet, in the face of it all, the world is devoting its talents, its energies, its resources, and its genius not to production, not for the things necessary to life, but for the things dedicated to destruction and death. In the midst of this Dantean hell of misery congresses and parliaments are busy, like the watchman upon his beat, hunting for some new thing to tax that more money may be extorted and more devilish instruments of torture may be perfected.

We seem to have two remedies for all this— levy more taxes and appropriate more money.

Everybody's face is turned, like the eastern worshipper, toward the Federal Treasury as his Mecca.

There is only one way to call a halt on these things. We can not do it through the Congress alone. The soldiers of this country can not be aided except as the country itself is rehabilitated. The soldier can not come back except the people as a whole come back.

The soldier can not prosper unless the people prosper. What good will it do the soldier to receive aid if by receiving it he depresses the value of the Liberty bond which his mother may have purchased or which his neighbor may have purchased or increases the taxes which his father must pay or his mother must pay or his neighbor must pay? He has now gone back and intermingled and become a part of the citizenship of the country; he is wrapped up in its welfare or in its adversity. The handing out to him of a few dollars will not benefit him under such circumstances, whereas it will greatly injure the prospects of the country and the restoration of normal conditions.

I know, of course, that there will be a vast amount of politics made with the matter, not only here but elsewhere; naturally that must follow; it is a part of the American game; we can not expect anything else; but I venture to believe that the young man who went to war, who was willing to sacrifice for his country, is just as much interested in the general welfare of his country as you or I, and that when the matter is presented to him and when he understands it, his patriotism, his manhood, his interest in mankind and in his fellows about him will guide him to a wise and patriotic conclusion. We need not be so uneasy as to the final judgment which he shall render.

If I may be permitted to say so, I desire to say that sometimes I think we underestimate the intelligence and patriotism of the masses of the American people. I think we sometimes find too much distress in telegrams and in letters which may not represent one-half of one per cent of the people in the community from which they come, and that we consider too little the fact that back there is the great reserve power, the reserved patriotism, the manhood upon which this Government rests, and upon which it must continue to rest or forever perish. If it is to be appealed to upon any occasion, we may safely appeal to it at a time when the whole country is bearing the burden which it is now bearing. And the soldier who was willing to serve his country when assailed from without will not be found wanting when his country needs him to adjust and rebuild her whole economic life within.

III

THE DISABLED SOLDIERS

(Excerpt from Speech of February 13, 1922.)

Mr. President, the disabled soldier stands out and apart from the rest of the citizens of the country, and is entitled to receive and does receive and will continue to receive the gracious consideration of his Government at all times. There is no difference of view, so far as I know, as to the obligation of the Government to equalize as nearly as it can the chances of the disabled soldier in the struggle of life. What we are doing and what we propose to do with reference to the disabled soldier is a matter of much concern and has its bearing upon the proposal of a bonus. The legislation which is proposed with reference to the soldier who has returned unimpaired in body or in mind will have its immediate bearing upon the ability and the willingness of the Government to discharge its obligations to the disabled soldier. It is, therefore, important to inquire what is the obligation which the Government assumes and which the Government must assume with reference to the disabled soldier and how will that obligation be affected by the legislation which is proposed with reference to general compensation. We can not dissociate the questions. One necessarily must have its bearing upon the other.

IV

TAXATION FOR THE BONUS

(Excerpt from Speech of July 6, 1922.)

I have called attention to this situation, which may seem somewhat irrelevant at first, but I am coming to the proposition of what should be the attitude of the American Congress toward these obligations which it is proposed we shall incur.

I look upon it somewhat in the light as if we were preparing for actual war. I think to drain our resources, to burden our people, to increase our obligations at this time is short-sighted, to say the least. It may be disastrous. It is a time when every citizen should feel toward his Government and its expenditures just as he would feel toward his Government if he knew that an outside enemy were threatening. Every man and every citizen should be willing to make the sacrifice, to economize, to deny himself or herself the same as we did during the Great War. There can be no possible doubt as to the task which confronts us, and there can be no doubt but what it will call for all we have under our control in order to meet it.

Notwithstanding that fact, we are told it is proposed as soon as this bill is out of the way to take up the ship subsidy bill. I am not going to discuss that today. I propose to do so in the near future. But it will be a drain upon the Treasury; it will establish a vicious system of tax exemption; it will not grant relief, and it will burden the future, in my judgment, quite as much as it would actually vote bonds or obligations of the Government.

Secondly, we propose to take up what is known as the soldiers' bonus bill. I am perfectly well aware that both sides of the Chamber are in favor of that proposition to a large extent. We are now paying out over $1,000,-000 a day for the disabled veterans; about $436,000,000 for this year will be paid, more than a million dollars a day. If we calculate the obligations which we owe to those men— and if they are disabled it is an obligation which we must meet at whatever cost—it will cost this Government, upon the ratio that it cost us after the Civil War, in the next fifty years over $65,000,000,000. Some estimate it higher. But, add that to the $22,000,000,000 which we already owe and the immense Budget which we have, and you have about all that the American taxpayer will be willing to carry during these coming years.

But it is proposed out of hand to lay upon the American people at this time an extra burden of from four to six billion dollars, almost twice as large as the debt which we had at the close of the Civil War; and if we pay it in the same way and at the same rate that we paid the debt after the Civil War, it will take us two hundred and fifty years to pay off the debt which we propose to lay in a few weeks for the purpose of this supposed obligation.

The discussion heretofore of this bonus measure has ranged principally about the present condition of the Federal Treasury and the immediate burdens of the taxpayer. These are matters of vital concern. But it must be apparent from the whole situation that underlying this question is a deeper problem touching not only this particular measure but the whole trend of legislation and the entire policy of reconstruction. The Treasury may run dry, but if the pride and the energy and the manhood and the womanhood of the Nation remain, it will again be replenished. The immediate burdens imposed by heavy taxes may sterilize industry and press down upon labor, but if faith in the Government and confidence in its policies remain, business in time will revive and labor again enjoy its rightful heritage. Language is inadequate to portray what a people will endure in the way of fiscal burdens so long as they believe that the policies obtaining are just and wise. But when a people begin to lose confidence in the wisdom and permanent policies of a government, it is time to look deeper than the mere significance of a pending measure.

The bonus measure is but a single expression of what seems to be a deep-rooted tendency—a tendency born of feeble policies and irresolute leadership. If this measure stood alone, if it were single in its import, we could look upon it with less concern. It is conspicuous, however, only because of the amount involved; there are any number of measures pending before the Congress of the same general nature. If you care to search the files of the Congress or survey the activities of State legislatures, you will no longer doubt the peril which confronts us as a people.

There are measures enough before the Congress, and lately in State legislatures, to bankrupt this, the richest Nation on the globe. If all the money were appropriated which, by bills, has been suggested, or if all the debts were created which such proposed measures would entail, it would place a mortgage upon the brain and the energy of our people which a thousand years could not lift. No statistician whom I have been able to find can tell us today the amount of indebtedness in the world. They approach with some supposed accuracy the debts of the different governments, but when you seek to tabulate the debts of the subdivisions of governments and then the private debts, the human mind staggers and computation breaks down. This fearful load resting like a blighting mildew upon the aspirations and the hopes and the energy of the people everywhere is now being increased at a rate which benumbs calculation. Even in this comparatively new land of ours we have reached already the era of embargoes, subsidies, gratuities, bonuses, and finally that sinister invention of American politics—50-50 between the States and the Government—that is, the States will exploit the taxpayer for 50 per cent and the Government for the other 50 per cent, thus dividing responsibility and augmenting extravagance, unmindful, apparently, that while the taxing power are two, the taxpayer in both instances is one and the same. The great task of legislation today is to ascertain how one class can benefit at the expense of another class —the taxpayer always the victim.

In times of adversity, in a severe economic crisis, a people, like individuals, must recur to first principles, return to the simple homely virtues, the only secure basis for either individual prestige or national power. Two roads were open to us and to all the world at the close of the Great War—that of waste, extravagance, taxes, and debts or that of economy, frugality, work, and self-denial.

The former leads inevitably to increased worry, greater misery, and ultimate ruin; the latter to contentment, prosperity, and strength. So far we have chosen the former course. When we have heard of unrest or political discontent, we have readily and generously tendered an appropriation. When the taxpayer has protested too earnestly, we have bravely put the burden upon posterity. Like economic cannibals, we are preying upon one another, and, going the cannibal one better, we are now preying upon our children and our children's children. Prosperity we assume is to come, not through individual sacrifice and individual effort, through self-exertion and personal initiative, but through the open door of the Public

Treasury. Although the sources of taxes are drying up, yet those who are not making their way from the Public Treasury with what they could get are wending their way toward it to see what is left. If I were going to open the Treasury to any people, or if I were going to support a continuance of this policy, I would not turn the soldier away. But the road over which we are traveling means industrial distress and ultimate disaster from which the soldier himself can not escape. People simply can not and will not much longer carry the load which we are imposing upon them. We have already tested their patience to the breaking point. The multitudes, it has been said, in all countries are patient to a certain point, but no statesman has ever yet been wise enough to foretell the particular point at which that patience ceases.

I grant you that if this policy is to continue there is no argument by which you can exclude the American soldier from participating in its temporary advantage; but it should also be said that there is no logic by which you can exclude him from its permanent disadvantages. No one is more deeply concerned in getting back to right principles and sound policies than these young men. No one is more vitally interested in the future welfare of the country. The unwisdom of the course we are now pursuing will fall more heavily upon these young men and theirs in coming years than upon those who are now in places of authority. It may be vain in this mad hour of political exigency and reckless appropriations to urge these views, but the inevitable hour will come when the soldier himself will regret, deeply regret, he ever consented to become a part of any such scheme. It may be idle —it may even be thought presumptuous— at this time to speak for a different standard, but I doubt not at all that in later years the soldier himself will rue the heedless hour when he exchanged a noble heritage for less than a mess of pottage. The thing which he gave, and stood ready to give, was without money and without price. The thing which he earned, the glory which was his, transcends the miserable values of the market. He does not rightfully belong in this futile scheme to rebuild civilization and reconstruct a bankrupt world through subsidies, bonuses, appropriations, taxes, and debts.

You will all recall the uneasiness, the anxiety, with which we followed the American soldier across the sea and onto the battle line in

Europe. He had been hurriedly called from the farm and the workshop, from school and college, and, practically unseasoned, undisciplined, and untrained, sent forward to meet the ordeal of war. His countrymen awaited the result with mingled feelings of fear and faith, and the whole world speculated on how he would meet the test.

We were told that this would be the real test of democracy—could a republic devoted to peace stand against the onslaught of centralized and thoroughly trained and highly militarized powers? We all know the result. The pride and the exultation we experienced over those first encounters of our troops no tongue can tell. They had met the test. They had vindicated our whole theory of government. They had justified our standard of civilization. They had checked and were soon to turn back the armies which had brought three great nations to bay. They had demonstrated that there was something after all higher and more masterful than sheer force—than mere organization. Behind the gun was character. Behind the weapons of destruction was unbought, unpurchasable love of country. Such service, sir, is the only security a republic can ever know. Such service spurns the idea of compensation, eludes all estimate, and defies the sordid rules of arithmetic. Let those disposed to do so trifle with the future by attempting to write across this glorious record "adjusted compensation."

But stern as was the task of the American soldier in war and unstinted as was the praise he won, a yet more inexorable obligation and a great opportunity awaited his return to civil life. The course which we are now pursuing will prove in the long run more dangerous to our Government than a foreign foe. A proud, strong nation may suffer a reverse in arms, but time may still find it triumphant. An independent and self-reliant people may be overcome by the fortunes of war, but time fights on their side to final victory. But a nation whose citizenship has been drugged and debauched by subsidies and gratuities and bonuses, who has surrendered to the excesses of a treasury orgy, has taken the road over which no nation has ever yet been able to effect a successful retreat.

Before we can come back as a people we must change our standards and adopt a different policy. Who will set up the new standards? Who will contend for the new policy? If these young men fail to do so, where shall we look for leadership? If great tasks and great opportunities be the things for which strong men yearn, this is the most coveted hour in the whole history of our Republic. The glory of Flanders Field and the deathless courage of Chateau-Thierry will not surpass the glory and the courage of the young men who see their duty and do it now.

The Great War threw back upon society its most stupendous task. Nothing like it in all the history of the world. The whole social and economic fabric had been shaken from center to circumference. Many of the most sacred traditions of the race, some of the most precious rights of the citizen, seemed imperiled. Old precedents were discredited. New policies were not at hand. To the ordinary citizen the world seemed steeped in debt, the future filled with drudgery and toil. It was a stricken world—hunger, disease, crime, suicide, insanity—stricken, it would seem, by one to whom alone vengeance belongs. But in spite of this fearful catastrophe the people bore up, carried the load with marvelously little complaint —carried it because they were promised on all hands and from every quarter by all political parties and all public servants that there was to be a new and nobler era in governmental affairs. Their interests were to be zealously guarded, sympathetically and vigilantly protected. We were all to cooperate to lift the load and lighten the burden. Are we keeping the promise made? Are we fulfilling the pledge? Are we lifting the burden? The faith of the citizen is after all the sole source of power in a free government. To destroy it is the most reckless offense of which the public servant can be guilty.

Is there any doubt, Mr. President, that there is a political revolution on in this country? We may not feel it in all its effects in Washington, but it has reached here to some extent. The people are resentful of the fact that the promises to lift the burden have not been kept. They are striking at men in office, in power, in order to reach systems and policies and programs. Business men are borrowing money to pay their taxes. I have examined the lists in ten of the great agricultural States of the Union and thousands of farms are for sale for taxes. While this condition confronts us, and while labor is dissatisfied and the farmer is discontented and business discouraged, we propose without hesitation, it seems, to lay upon the American people an additional burden of from $4,000,000,000 to $6,000,000,000.

The Republican Party is now in power.

Others may vote with the party to lay on these increased taxes and burdens, but the responsibility is fixed and inescapable; it is with the party to whom has been intrusted the reins of authority. For the sake of our common country, for the sake of peace and happiness among the millions who must bear the awful load, who can not pass it on, will not the old party of so many noble victories rise to meet the occasion and stop once and for all this orgy of extravagance, this saturnalia of expenditure, until the people can redeem our country from discontent and strife and bring it back to prosperity and power?

V

LINCOLN THE ORATOR

(Address delivered at Lincoln's Birthplace, November 9, 1911. The subject, "Lincoln the Orator," was assigned to the speaker by the committee having in charge the dedication of Lincoln farm.)

The life of no other public man is so well and so universally known as that of Abraham Lincoln. The hovel in which he was born, the loneliness of his childhood days, the poverty of his early manhood, the improvident and restless father, the sweet face which tradition gives his mother, the self-discipline, the hunger for knowledge, the rise from obscurity to power, the singular judgment and remarkable wisdom with which he exercised that power, his honesty, his great tenderness of heart, the marvel of his eloquence, the tragic close—these are the meager outlines of an epic from the simple homely life of American democracy, and the 'American people love and cherish it one and all, North and South. Fiction has no story so interesting as this. Poetry has not clothed its heroes with a mastery won over such obstacles and yet so complete as that which plain truth reveals in the sad and solitary career of this marvelous man.

Our government calls for a dual capacity in statesmanship—a combination of the apostle and the lawgiver. To frame and to successfully enact and execute our laws demands a high order of intellect; it involves a clear and comprehensive insight into the mechanism of our institutions. But there is another work which we can not neglect. So long as all sovereignty rests with the people, so long as the enactment of good laws and the enforcement of all law depend so largely upon the intelligence and conscience of the citizen, we cannot dispense with those who speak with wisdom and power to the multitude. Such are the men who keep alive that eternal vigilance which is the price of all we have. They are the tribunes of the people. Without them the public conscience would become sluggish and the wisest measures sometimes fail. They arouse public interest. They organize public thought. They call forth and direct the invincible moral forces of an entire nation. There is no higher duty than that of arousing to moderate and sustained action the minds of those with whom all power rests. There can be no graver responsibility than that of directing the people in the use of the instrumentalities of government.

Oratory has always been a factor in great

movements. Spoken thought has been controlling in more than one crisis of human rights. There has seldom been a time when men were not to be moved to great deeds through the power of eloquence. It has been at times a most potent influence in the cause of liberty. If the time ever comes when it shall no longer have that influence, as many are fond to prophesy, it will be after selfishness and sensuality shall have imbruted or destroyed all the nobler faculties of the mind. The people have at different periods in their bewilderment and travail, when old beliefs were passing and old institutions crumbling, waited for some great leader, rich in human sympathy, to speak with that uncommon power with which it is given few men to speak. Lincoln was undoubtedly one of those few. He came from no school. He was the pride of no university. In spite of many obstacles he came to his own. Without the advantage of wealth, leisure or family prestige he outstripped all competitors. Accident or environment, necessity or chance may modify and color the fabric of life, yet purpose and will are masters also of these, and the strong and purposeful youth arose from his harsh and obscure surroundings to become the unchallenged voice of one of the most righteous of the world's great movements.

The first qualification of an orator is that he be master of his subject. The second, that his subject be master of him. This was singularly true with reference to Lincoln. His lyceum lectures and his speeches upon ordinary occasions do not rise above the commonplace. It was when the blight of slavery threatened the free soil of the North that his latent powers were given the energy and sweep of genius. This strange, untrained voice laden with sympathy but firm in tone rang through the land, tugging continuously at the consciences of men until the lethargy and selfishness of a century melted and fell away. He aroused public sentiment. He marshalled the righteousness of the nation. He crystallized the best there was in men, directed it through the channels of government, and at last embodied it into laws and constitutions. Through the power of speech he, more than anyone else, set in motion the moral forces which disenthralled a race. In the affairs of government and in the details of diplomacy he ranks among the great Presidents. But in this faith of ours which we call democracy he stands apart, its voice and conscience—a great apostolic figure Who reads today his speech at Gettysburg, his second inaugural address or the letter to the brave mother who had lost five sons in battle, not to feel, to realize that here was a political gospel worthy of the faith which we profess, commensurate with the destiny for which as a people we strive. In no other do we find such an unqualified acceptance of the basic truths of popular government.

The scholar with his wide range of words, his brilliant rhetoric, stood on the field of Gettysburg, beside the man whose school days could have been measured by the days of a single year. The one was the fruit of five generations of New England culture, the other took his diploma from the "university of nature." The one had mastered the logic of the books, the other understood perfectly the logic of the human heart. The one, slavish to his great art, clothed his theme in all the witchery of his inimitable style. The other, burdened with sorrow for those who had there given "the last full measure of their devotion," spoke with the abandon of a sorely chastened and overwrought mind. The one had an oration, the other a message. The one was rhetoric, the other eloquence. It is after all by reason of a profound conviction or the anguish of an all absorbing moral passion born amid the storms and tempests which sometimes sweep the soul that the heights of true oratory are obtained. Learning, culture, the training of the schools will aid, but these alone will not suffice. Paul before Agrippa, Phillips conquering the mob, O'Connell lifting a down-trodden people to the dignity of a nation, Burke aroused by the long line of indefensible crimes of Hastings, Webster pleading for the Union, Lincoln voicing the nation's compassion and the nation's courage at Gettysburg—these are the occasions and the themes which fuse and mould into one majestic and harmonious whole the varied powers of the gifted mind.

It is natural in speaking of Mr. Lincoln as an orator to recur to the occasions such as the second inaugural or the dedication of the field of Gettysburg, occasions upon which he spoke with such tenderness and pathos, such feeling, fitness and eloquence, such simple yet such searching power. But we cannot take his full measure as a public speaker without considering the great debate. This was the most crucial test of pure intellect to which he was ever subjected, for Stephen A. Douglas was "no mean" antagonist, no ordinary man. Endowed by nature with unusual mental power

he had had the advantage of years of association with the strong minds of a most stirring
period and a wide experience in the halls of
legislation.   Bold, resourceful, ambitious, he
had no superior and few equals as a debater in
the Senate of the United States, of which he
was then the most interesting and striking figure.   At the time of the debate he was at the
very zenith of his popularity and in the full
and imperious possession of all his great powers, both natural and acquired.   He went into
the contest with the spirit of victory strong
upon him and inspired by the devotion of fol-
lowers who thought it was not his to lose. The
debate, as we know, took place in the open air
in the presence of thousands of anxious follow-
ers.   The theme, the surroundings, the momentous consequences which all dimly foresaw as
soon to follow—for each spoke to and for a distinct civilization—make this debate unique,
exceptional and profoundly interesting even
now and must have made it vastly more interesting and absorbing to those who listened or
who read of it as it progressed.

In the give and take of the close grip of the
contest, in the finesse and brilliant fencing
which sometimes seem essential in that kind of
a deadly intellectual encounter, in the adroit

and telling display of points for immediate effect before the great throng Douglas seems the superior. But in the calm and lucid statement of principles, in the remorseless arrangement of a great subject in order to hurl it with final effect upon the listener, in the use of that logic which is born of the wedlock of conscience and intellect, in the capacity to read out of the future the result of today's policies, in the prophetic sweep of a great mind, Lincoln was distinctly and unquestionably far the superior of his adversary. In fact, the great qualities which Lincoln possessed Douglas, with all his genius for debate, did not possess at all. There was no chance in such a duel of intellects for the false or specious arts of oratory. Each realized that "economy of expression" and integrity of thought must take the place of the diffuse and superficial entertainments with which men are prone to entertain popular assemblies. Never was more profound respect paid to the intelligence and patriotism of the people. I do not know of another figure in all the history of our free institutions so impressive as that of Lincoln as he stood before these vast throngs conducting his great propaganda of righteousness, and I do not know of one who ever spoke with greater power and effect.

The number of our public men who have sincerely accepted in full the principles of a democratic or republican form of government has not been so large as we sometimes suppose. Some of the ablest were never able to be free from an honest distrust in the self-governing capacity of those whom we so often style the common people. But Lincoln's faith in our institutions and in the power of the people to rule was natural, simple and sincere. He had been and always continued to be one of them. Born in that lowly sphere where the anthem of human sympathy enriches the heart of childhood with compassion for all he learned to read the human heart, knew its emotions, its hopes and its longings far better than he knew books. But his speeches are wholly free from the protestations of loyalty to the people which so often characterize the addresses of public leaders. The insinuating and subtle self-laudation of an Alcibiades is in his speeches nowhere to be found. In all his public utterances there is no appeal to prejudice, no effort to mislead. Moderation is the constant surprise of every reader of his speeches—a rare quality indeed in political addresses. He never mistook anger for righteousness. In him there was nothing of the demagogue. He did not flatter, and in passion's hour he did not follow. He possessed in a remarkable way the capacity for intellectual solitude, even in the midst of the throng—yet he never lost faith in the throng. He paid the people the high compliment of speaking to them in the language of reason and true eloquence. He believed they would accept a great principle as a controlling basis for action, and time proved he was not mistaken. Some speakers seem to think it necessary to shriek, to exaggerate, to impugn, to resort to the cheap and common arts of public speaking when talking to the people at large. Lincoln never offered this challenge to their intelligence and manhood.

It is such qualities as these which make it difficult to speak of Lincoln as an orator or Lincoln as a lawyer or Lincoln as a political leader. There was in him a fulness, a completeness, a greatness, which seem to forbid an attempt to accentuate particular qualities. In the consideration of particular elements of strength we are soon lost in the contemplation of his massive figure as a whole. His life in all its wretchedness and glory, in all its penury and power intrudes itself upon us and seems as inexplicable and incomprehensible as the cunning of Angelo's chisel or the touch of

Titian's brush. Sacred writers, had he lived in those days, would have placed him among their seers and prophets and invested him with the hidden powers of the mystic world. Antiquity would have clothed such a being with the attributes of deity. He was one of the moral and intellectual giants of the earth.

But we do not attempt to describe a painting of one of the old masters before which we stand in wonder and admiration. Millions feel the inspiration of a great character, just as they feel the inspiration and thrill of a great poem, but in no wise seek or hope to tell the secret of the influence or power over them. We are dealing today as millions have dealt for fifty years with the life of one whose name and memory all revere. But even the most superlative masters of expression have not as yet portrayed in all its fulness the ever-growing greatness of his name. We see the awkward country boy in his cabin home in the midst of the trackless forest. We see him cover his mother's grave with winter's withered leaves and return to his cabin home to unconsciously enter the race for fame. We see him as he walks near the auction block in the slave market and hear his almost weird curse pronounced upon the institution of slavery. We see him in after years, when as the greatest ruler upon this earth, he walked with patience and compassion the paths of power—we hear men denounce him as a tyrant and a murderer while patiently he submits to it all. At last the storm begins to clear, the light breaks through the rifted clouds and we see him walking in the dawn of a new day and four million human beings are there unloosed of their fetters—and then the altar and the sacrifice. It seems like an exaggerated tale of oriental fancy, but it is not. The story is the product of our own soil. It is what happened here among a clean, liberty loving people, under the inspiration of our free institutions. It was and is in the fullest sense the guarantee which God and God alone gave, and, as we must believe every hour, gives, that no matter what the test, a government "conceived in liberty and dedicated to the proposition that all men are created equal shall not perish from the earth."

VI

THE NEED FOR RESTRICTED IMMIGRATION

Senator Borah's attitude is revealed by this argument made as far back as 1916, nine months before America entered the World War. It has since become, in large measure, that of the Republican administration. The excerpts are from a speech in the United States Senate.

The immigration bill which is now upon the calendar has passed Congress twice substantially in its present form. It passed Congress by an overwhelming vote in both instances. It was vetoed twice. * * * I regard the bill as of the utmost importance. It is important in its bearings and in its effect, and would be so at any time and under any conditions which obtain in this country; but it is peculiarly important by reason of the conditions which, in my judgment, will prevail at the close of the great conflict now going on in Europe. We ought to have our fences up and be thoroughly prepared to protect those in this country who will be brought into competition with the hordes of people who will come here, in my judgment, at the close of the war. No subject could more concern or better engage this Congress than that of protecting our laborers and our country in general against the conditions which will then confront us.

We have prepared for other contingencies and conditions. We have provided an ample Navy and, in the judgment of some, a fairly well organized land force. It is just as important—indeed, sir, I think more important—that we should prepare for peace, for the industrial conditions which shall confront us when the war shall have closed. We can never acquit our full obligations to the working people of this country and to our citizenship if we adjourn this Congress without action in this particular.

We all hope that the battleships which we are going to build will never be put in actual use, that they will rot unused upon the sea. It is our hope that any Army for which we may have provided may never be called into action; and it is reasonably probable that neither of these forces will be called into actual use. But the conditions which will confront us at the close of the war are inevitable. We can not escape from the situation as it will then be developed. Whatever may be the result as to the other preparedness, whether it shall be necessary as we have contemplated it or not, the preparedness for industrial peace and industrial conditions is necessary.

It seems to me, Mr. President, after having devoted so much time to the other forms of preparedness, it would be well if we would take up this measure and meet a real emergency and deal with a real condition, and undertake to ameliorate and control a real situation which will confront and environ and embarrass every man who labors at whatever calling it may be in this country. * * *

It is an astounding situation that a bill which has twice passed Congress by an overwhelming majority and has in this Chamber such unanimous support should be postponed even for a week. It is a situation which does not speak in complimentary terms of the most distinguished deliberative body, as we are fond of saying, in the world. It presents to us the question whether or not we are dealing in candor and in courage with a situation which we know to be real. It does not speak in complimentary terms of this body, knowing the situation as we know it and the conditions which will confront the laboring men of this country at the close of the war, if we postpone or trifle with the situation or with a measure designed to ameliorate that situation to some extent at least. In the name of candor and fair dealing, in the name of honor, among public men let us place duty above supposed party expediency.

If there were a divided Senate, if there were a divided sentiment here to any great extent in regard to it, it might be said that there would be interminable debate and possibly defeat in the end; but, I repeat, I doubt if there are ten Senators in this Senate Chamber who are opposed to the bill to the extent that they would vote against it if the bill should be brought to a final vote. Surely so important a measure is entitled to consideration; surely men will not side-step or dodge this kind of an issue.

It is the history of all great wars that large immigration follows immediately after the struggle is over. I said the history of all great wars; I should have said of wars in Europe. It has been almost invariably the rule that when the conflict shall have closed there is a large emigration from the regions of country over which the conflict was waged.

I shall not detain the Senate in going back and recounting those instances, but every Senator will recall them. It is for the reason that war disturbs the family relations, breaks up old friendships, pulls men out of the grooves to which they are accustomed and puts them in another line of life; for the reason that the country in which their homes were situated may have been scourged by war, the discouragement and disappointment environing the man as he leaves his regiment or his army and starts back to his home, and he naturally seeks a place where he may begin life under different conditions, where he may seize if possible new opportunities, and especially where he may escape what he believes to be conditions which it is not within his power as an individual to molify or overcome. He is restless for other climes, and all places seem better than the place cursed by the memory of his sacrifices.

Then again, when this great war shall have closed the tremendous debt which will be hanging over those belligerent countries will be a warning to every man of whatever station of life or of whatever occupation, that for years and years, for him and his children and his children's children, there is to be that depressing weight upon him and his in the struggle of life. The debt which will exist at the close of the war no one can estimate, but it is now running up to where it is estimated at about fifty to sixty billion dollars. Who can estimate the misery, the sorrow, the sacrifice involved in the fact that those belligerent countries after the cannon shall cease to roar will have fastened upon the labor of those countries, upon the industry of the countries, such an insuperable, almost inconceivable burden which must be paid at last through the toil and sacrifice of the man in the street, in the mines, and in the factory. From this they will seek to escape as from some slow consuming curse.

Do not mistake that those in the ordinary walks of life understand that just as well as those in the higher walks of life who undertake to deal with high finance. Even if they do not appreciate it as those more trained in that mysterious science appreciate it, yet its nebulous undefined menace comes to them with more force for the reason that they can scarcely comprehend it than if they could weigh and analyze and devise schemes and means by which it could finally be liquidated. All they understand is that it is there and must be met by taxes for which they must suffer.

So these things and a multitude more will encourage every man who is not fastened in some way to the land of his birth to seek new fields and new opportunities, and where will they go? To what country will they turn their face? Toward the great Republic of the West, and they will come in direct competition with the men in this country just so surely as time goes on. Now, sir, in so far as practicable I would alleviate those conditions, but I can not get my consent to do so at the cost of hunger and destitution, of the misery and sacrifice of our own people.

But that is not all. There is a deeper and a broader question involved, and that it is obligatory upon every generation, and particularly upon this, in view of the tremendous conditions prevailing in Europe, to protect the citizenship of this country, to keep up the average standard of citizenship, that this great Republic of ours may rest in safety upon the shoulders not of the few, not of the public men alone, but upon the shoulders of the average man, for there and there alone is the foundation rock upon which this Republic must rest in every crisis. If I could feel that our laws and the administration of our laws were in the future to be such as would be conducive to the health and morals, the prosperity and happiness, of the average citizen of our country I would feel confident, wholly confident, of the future. This country will never be wanting in the ability of individual men, in intellectual power, but it may be wanting in justice, in that equitable distribution of this world's wealth and this world's blessings essential to a sound and wholesome democracy.

Why should we delay? Why should we postpone the consideration of a measure that has now received the commendation and common judgment of the representatives of the people upon two separate occasions, and would receive it again if some mysterious, subtle, indefinable, inscrutable, incomprehensible power were not preventing its consideration? The question before this Congress is not, Is this bill wise or just that we have settled? But the question is, Shall we have the courage to challenge the power which opposes its passage?

It is said that so many people will have been slaughtered in the war that we need have no fear. I was enlightened a few weeks ago by reading an editorial in one of the great metropolitan dailies to the effect that there would be no occasion for immigration laws after the war shall have closed; that there would be such a sacrifice of life that we must necessarily conclude there would be no occasion for an undue amount of immigration in this country. There is in those belligerent countries a population estimated at 450,000,000. If we make the estimate according to the ordinary rule, that would give us in those belligerent countries 90,000,000 working people; rather I should say 90,000,000 adult people, and according to the ordinary estimate 80 per cent of the adults perform labor in some way, occupy themselves in the industrial world so that they may be classed as laborers. That leaves about 72,000,000 adult workingmen in those countries. Suppose we assume that even 10,000,000 shall have been sacrificed in this war, we still have 62,000,000 of workingmen in the belligerent countries alone. Then we have this other fact which they refuse to consider, that the women of those countries have passed into the lines of industry and taken the place of the men until you have practically the entire vacancy, as it were, caused by the enlistment of men supplied by the women workers of those countries. And when we contemplate the tremendous output of the industries of those countries, how fully and completely labor is meeting the situation, how can we doubt that the close of the war and the return from the field of war will find an over-crowded labor field?

You will not at the close of this war have any less workmen, including the women, than you had in these countries at the beginning of the war, notwithstanding the sacrifice. You have the men, the women, and the children, and you have those countries driving those working people to the limit to win back the markets of the world. The situation will not be mollified, we should not suppose it will be mollified, by the unfortunate sacrifice which will be made in this war.

A few days ago we passed what is called the child-labor bill, supposedly, and I hope, a humanitarian piece of legislation. But suppose that we shall have succeeded in taking the child out of the factory, in depriving it, even amid most uninviting environments and adverse conditions, of its opportunity to work; suppose we shall have taken it from the surroundings which we believe to be calculated to arrest its development and to circumscribe its life and send it to a home of squalor and want and misery—to what extent have we served humanity? Suppose we shall have taken the child out of the factory and sent it to a home where we have, by reason of our immigration laws, deprived the father or mother of a job, displaced some one else occupying the position of those upon whom it is dependent for support. If the parents of this country, the mother and the father are not to be protected in their citizenship, if they are not to be protected in their wage or in their place, we shall have exerted an impotent but ostentatious display of legislative power in taking the child from the factory.

It is incumbent upon this Congress to supplement that legislation by such legislation as will protect the home to which the child is supposed to return and to give its parents their prestige and their place in the industrial world, where they may educate and take care of the child. Otherwise, Mr. President, in attempting to serve humanity we have pursued an ignis fatuus; we have harmed the child instead of helped it.

I gave notice at one time that I should offer the immigration bill as an amendment to the child-labor bill, and a distinguished Senator upon the floor, who is absent now, and the newspapers of the country, to a considerable extent, and especially those who were greatly engrossed in the child-labor legislation, said that there was no kith or kin between these two measures and they should not be in any way embarrassed one by the other.

Is there no relationship between the child in the factory under adverse circumstances and the child who returns home and is turned upon the streets to vagrancy and incipient crime by reason of the fact that its father or its mother may have been reduced in wage by the severer competition which is sure to follow, or even displaced entirely? While I have the utmost sympathy and consideration for the child working in the factory under conditions which may arrest its development and unfit it for citizenship, as between the child in those conditions and the child living upon the streets to the point of vagrancy I have more profound sympathy for the latter.

But, Mr. President, there are some influences which are being exerted against the immigration bill which were not exerted against the child-labor bill. The evils of child labor were said to be confined to five or six States. It is easy, Mr. President, to make an ostentatious display of your humanitarianism when it is at the expense of somebody across the line. But this immigration bill, sir, has its opposition more disseminated throughout the entire country. It affects powerful interests; it affects those who make large contributions to campaign funds; it affects powerful interests in every part of the country; and, therefore, we hesitate and halt in the protection of the mother and the father while we parade our humanitarianism by taking care of the child. I say, sir, we shall have acted the part of hypocrites if we take that child from the factory, unwholesome and dangerous as its surroundings may be, and turn it upon the street to beg or steal because we have failed to protect the workman's home.

When the European war broke out what was the condition of labor in this country? On the 1st day of August, 1914, according to statistics now accepted—and which have become so well accepted as to be beyond the charge of political manufacture—there were out of employment in this country 2,500,000 men. Who has the power to describe the condition which those figures indicate—2,500,000 men out of employment, struggling upon the ragged edge of hunger, with their children asking them for support and for the means which it is not within their power to supply?

But suppose I should be in error and that I overdraw the picture. It reminds me of a statement made by a distinguished divine, who said that if a man accepted and believed the Christian religion, and it turned out to be baseless, no harm was done; but that if a man rejected it, and it turned out to be true, it would undoubtedly be of dire consequences to him.

If I should be in error as to the situation which will then confront us, perhaps this bill would not be so necessary; but if I should be correct, and if others should be correct in regard to it, it is supremely important; it is eminently essential to the welfare and to the happiness of millions of people of this country.

Why delay? Why postpone? Whom are we going to deceive when the election is over? If we postpone this thing until the 2d day of December, 1916, who is going to be disappointed after the election is over? Whom are we getting ready to betray? Let us have it before the great judgment is recorded. Let us hew to the line, let the chips fall where they may. One party has just as much interest as the other, and one party is calculated to lose just as much as the other. To postpone it until after election is such a manifest and diaphanous scheme of duplicity that I am amazed at the boldness of men who propose it.

I wish to take a few minutes to read, in support of the contentions which I have made, some views of others with reference to this situation. I read from the Independent, under date of May 8, 1916, an article by Isaac Don Levine. He says:

There has been a great deal of discussion in this country since the war began about the volume of immigration to the United States after the restoration of peace in Europe. There are those who argue that conditions in the Old World will be such after the war is over that there will hardly be any increase in the present rate of immigration, which is negligible. But the overwhelming number of authorities on immigration, among whom are the numerous representatives of immigrant aid societies, as well as most of the United States immigration officials, are of the opinion that immigration to this country after the war will assume unprecedented proportions.

It may be safely said now that this latter view has come to be generally recognized as the right one. Those who believe that for years to come this country will know no immigration problem disregard economic conditions. They hope for an era of marvelous recuperation and reconstruction in Europe, an attractive hope, but hardly justified by reason. * * *

*   *   *   *   *   *   *   *   *

I read portions of an article from the Scientific Monthly of May, 1916, by Prof. Robert DeC. Ward of Harvard University:

No one who has at heart the future of the American race can fail to view with concern the probable effects of the war upon the physical, mental, and moral condition of our immigrants. The introduction of pestilential war diseases, such as cholera, typhus, typhoid fever, and the like is not greatly to be feared, although some of our medical men are already viewing this problem with much concern. On the other hand, the more subtle and much less easily detected venereal diseases, which are always rampant in great armies in war time, and the mental breakdowns, of which there are so many thousands of cases among the soldiers at the front, present another aspect of the health problem which is far more serious. Great numbers of soldiers, although not actually afflicted with any specific disease, will eventually come to the United States maimed, crippled, wounded, enfeebled by illness or exposure, or mentally unstable. The fittest mentally and physically, those who in the past have had the initiative and the courage to emigrate will be dead at the prime of life or will be needed at home to carry on the work of rebuilding and reorganization. These are the men whom Europe will do its utmost to keep at home. The least fit are likely to emigrate.

Many of those who, because of mental or physical disability, will find themselves least able to earn a living abroad, will be the very ones most likely to be "assisted" by relatives and friends in this country to "come to America." Against the emigration of such persons the European Governments will not set up any barriers. There are good grounds, therefore, for expecting, with reasonable certainty, that our immigration in the next few decades after the war will be of a lower physical and mental standard than it has been in the past.

I shall not detain the Senate longer in the discussion of this matter, nor longer delay the passage of this important measure which is now before the Senate. I understand we are to vote upon it this afternoon, and I have no desire to delay it; but I think I have called attention to sufficient facts and to the opinions of those whose views are worthy to be considered, to show the importance of this immigration measure, not only to the immediate laborers of the country but to the entire community, the Republic as a whole.

If it should be determined in the future, by actual occurrences, that the situation is not so bad as contemplated, nor so imminent as it seems at this time, still there is abundant argument adduced heretofore many times, never answered, irrefutable, for the passage of the bill. Aside from the extraordinary conditions and the exceptional situation, there are the fundamental principles upon which the bill is based which have warranted its passage heretofore and ought to justify its consideration now. I have not gone back into those principles. I have thought it well to deal with what I conceive to be exceptional and imminent conditions. I am most profoundly impressed with the belief that the highest duty of this Congress is to meet them as effectively as it is within the power of faithful public servants to do. If we go away without doing so it will be shameless betrayal of a most serious and solemn obligation.

In conclusion, let me say to the Senator from Georgia [Mr. Hardwick], who sits near me, and who has advised me of the purpose of the Senator from South Carolina [Mr. Smith], that there can be no possible way of preventing the passage of this measure if the Senator from South Carolina will make his motion and the Senators in this body who believe in this bill will cast their votes in accordance with their convictions. There is just one influence which can defeat this measure, and no other, and that is the caucus of the majority, which makes or unmakes legislation here. If you will take the grip of King Caucus off the consciences and convictions of the men who sit in this body, this transcendent measure will become the expression of this body before the session closes; and what I ask now, that it may be recorded in unmistakable terms, is whether this body is to legislate or whether the caucus is to strangle?

VII

FREE SPEECH

(Excerpt from speech in the United States Senate, April 19th, 1917.)

So much, Mr. President, for the legal phase of this matter. I want to say a few words in regard to the policy of it. I suppose it will be conceded that here we are all Americans and thoroughly in accord with the idea that we should leave nothing undone which we can do properly or wisely to prevent information reaching those with whom we are at war. I assume that no one could for a moment in this Chamber harbor the idea that we should loosely permit information to go to the enemy which might be of benefit to him. I would want to go as far as one would need to go in order to protect that situation; but evil of that kind is not commensurate in its import with the evil which might flow from an abridgement of the freedom of the press.

Edwin Burke once said:

It is right that there should be a clamor whenever there is an abuse. The fire bell at midnight disturbs your sleep, but it keeps you from being burned in your bed. The hue

61

and cry alarms the country, but it preserves all the property of the Province.

We may suppose ourselves capable of seeing the evils of a free press or free speech, but it is almost impossible to even outline in the way of suggestions the benefits of a free press and free speech. Hence the wisdom of the ages is that we should permit unrestrained use of the printed page and speech and punish alone for abuse.

Sir James McIntosh in the Peltier case observed as follows:

To inform the public on the conduct of those who administer public affairs requires courage and conscious security. It is always an invidious and obnoxious office, but it is often the most necessary of all public duties. If it is not done boldly, it can not be done effectually, and it is not from writers trembling under the uplifted scourge that we are to hope for it.

How exceedingly wise! What is the press or speech worth if fear, indefinite power to punish, ever accompany the use?

Lord Northcliffe by publications in England stirred the nation from center to circumference, exposed the ineptitude—the almost criminal ineptitude—of some who had charge of the nation's affairs. Could he not have been punished under this bill? Will anyone contend that the London Times, in the days when Lord Northcliffe was revolutionizing the situation with reference to the fighting forces of England, could have been published under this proposed statute? Does anyone doubt that if Lord Northcliffe had not made those publications in all probability the English Army would have broken down or suffered incalculably? Has there been a greater and more distinct service rendered to the cause of English arms than has been rendered by the English press? All this would undoubtedly have been inhibited under this provision of this proposed statute.

Go back to another service performed by the London Times in the Crimean War. The publications made by that paper at that time not only changed for the better the situation with reference to the contest and mercilessly exposed those who were incapable of carrying the arms to success, but so exposed the aristocracy of England in its criminal incapacity that it was the initiatory step in the great democratic movement in England which led to the enfranchisement of the people 10 years afterwards.

I could come closer home for illustrations, but it would perhaps be a breach of taste to do so.

Mr. President, in this struggle of democracy, in this crusade for free institutions, let us hold fast among ourselves to those great underlying principles of freedom and liberty without which we may be a Republic in name, but could never be one in fact. Without an unfettered press, without liberty of speech, all the outward forms and structures of free institutions are a sham, a pretense—the sheerest mockery. If the press is not free; if speech is not independent and untrammeled; if the mind is shackled or made impotent through fear, it makes no difference under what form of government you live you are a subject and not a citizen. Republics are not in and of themselves better than other forms of government except in so far as they carry with them and guarantee to the citizen that liberty of thought and action for which they were established.

Of all times in time of war the press should be free. That of all occasions in human affairs calls for a press vigilant and bold, independent and uncensored. Better to lose a battle than to lose the vast advantage of a free press. A free and independent press, as historic incidents show, may be of greater service than any other single feature of a great conflict.

In times of war corruption and venality, sordidness and greed are always active, always prevalent. I know of very few exceptions. It was so in the Civil War when the Union seemed to be going to pieces. It was true—notoriously and brazenly true—during the Spanish-American War. Men were fed on diseased food that greed might riot in its profits. Everywhere, in high places and low places, men were spying about for a chance to take advantage of the patriotic people engaged in defending the honor of their country. I know of nothing more important to a free people in time of war, in time of great stress, than a free press.

I think one of the greatest services we can render the cause of democracy just now is to demonstrate to the world that a Republic can carry on war, defend itself effectively and triumphantly without recurring to the practices and procedures of absolute governments. The most interesting and at the same time the saddest features of this war to me, aside from the suffering and sacrifices of those engaged, has been the haste with which the freer, more liberal governments have adopted the arbitrary and dictatorial policies and practices of the most absolute of governments. There are no democracies at this hour in this conflict, whatever may be the outward form or whatever the fact was before the war, and whatever the fact may be after the war. It is certainly not for me to suggest that things could have been otherwise and that these arbitrary and absolute measures were unnecessary, for I have no reason to challenge the good faith of those who have risked all in this struggle. But I am sure if the time is to come when we shall have to follow in that course that time has not yet arrived. I do not believe that time will ever come. I think if danger should become more imminent and the situation more perilous that the patriotism, the active and self-imposed censorship of the press will meet in full the demands of the hour. I think the individual citizen will measure up to the occasion. I at least want to try out this situation to the end and see if a Republic may not be a Republic in war as well as a Republic in peace. I shall not have much faith in our institutions if they are fitted only to sail in serene seas and wholly unable to withstand the storm.

VIII

AMERICANISM

(Speech in the United States Senate, February 21, 1919.)

Mr. President, the people of the United States have the undoubted right to change their form of government and to renounce established customs or long-standing policies whenever in their wisdom they see fit to do so. As a believer in democratic government, I readily acknowledge the right of the people to make in an orderly fashion such changes as may be approved in their judgment at any time. I contend, moreover, that when radical and important departures from established national policies are proposed, the people ought to be consulted.

We are now proposing what to my mind is the most radical departure from our policies hitherto obtaining that has ever been proposed at any time since our Government was established. I think the advocates of the league will agree with me that it is a pronounced departure from all the policies which we have heretofore obtained.

It may be wise, as they contend; nevertheless, it involves a different course of conduct upon the part of the Government and of our people for the future, and the people are entitled to pass judgment upon the advisability of such a course.

It seems clear, also, that this proposed program, if it is to be made effective and operative under the proposed constitution of the league, involves a change in our Constitution. Certainly, questions of that kind ought to be submitted to a plebiscite or to a vote of the people, and the Constitution amended in the manner provided for amending that instrument. We are merely agents of the people; and it will not be contended that we have received any authority from the principal, the people, to proceed along this line. It is a greater responsibility than an agent ought to assume without express authority or approval from his principal to say nothing of the want of authority. Preliminary to a discussion of this question, therefore, I want to declare my belief that we should arrange the machinery for taking a vote of the people of the United States upon this stupendous program. I am aware that the processes by which that may be accomplished involve some difficulties; but they are not insurmountable, and they are by no means to be compared in their difficulty with the importance of being right, and in harmony with the judgment of the people before we proceed to a final approval. We should have the specific indorsement of those whose agents we are and we should have the changes in our Constitution that we may have sanction under the Constitution for the fearful responsibility we propose to assume. If we can effectuate this change now proposed without direct authority from the people I can not think of a question of sufficient moment to call for their indorsement.

It must be conceded that this program can never be a success unless there is behind it the intelligent and sustained public opinion of the United States. If the voters do not have their voice before the program is initiated, they will certainly have an opportunity to give expression to their views in the future. They are still the source of power, and through their votes they effectuate the policies under which we must live. From the standpoint, therefore, of expediency and from the standpoint of fairness to those who are most concerned, to wit, the people, those who must carry the burdens, if there be burdens, and suffer the consequences, if there should be ill consequences to suffer, as well as from the standpoint of insuring success, if possible, the mass of the people ought to be consulted and their approval had before we proceed. I, therefore, in the very beginning of this procedure, declare in favor of that program.

I think I should have deferred any remarks I had to make upon this subject until a later day, had it not been for an interview which was put out by Mr. Taft some two or three days ago upon this question. I felt, in view of that statement, that those who were opposed to the program were justified in proceeding at once to the debate, because it is a statement which in my judgment is not founded upon fact. In saying that I do not charge a conscious purpose upon the part of Mr. Taft to mislead, but I am sure it can not be sustained by the historic facts at the command of anyone who desires to examine the subject; and as it can not be sustained, it is to the utmost degree misleading.

Mr. Taft informs the American people, from the pedestal of an ex-President, that this program does not destroy the policy announced by Washington in his Farewell Address and does not renounce the doctrine known as the

Monroe doctrine—two fundamental principles underlying our foreign policy for more than one hundred years in one instance and nearly one hundred years in the other; two policies to which the American people have long been committed, and which, in my judgment, they still believe to be indispensable to their happiness and future tranquillity. If, indeed, this program does dispose of these policies, it presents an entirely different question to the American people than if the reverse were true. This is one of the first things to be settled in this controversy. It meets us at the very threshold of all discussion and all consideration. It is of such moment as to call for clear statement and candid presentation. What is the effect of this proposed program upon these ancient and most vital policies?

Mr. Taft says:

Article 10 covers the Monroe doctrine and extends it to the world. * * * The league is to be regarded as in conflict with the advice of Washington only with a narrow and reactionary viewpoint.

"Reactionary" is not a familiar term in the ex-President's vocabulary. I think he has unintentionally misused it.

Mr. President, prior to the administration of Washington, America had been involved in every European war since colonization began. When a difficulty arose in Europe, whatever might be the subject of the difficulty, whether dynastic quarrels or territorial aggrandizement, it spread at once to the American Continent. Although we might be wholly unconcerned in the controversy upon its merits, nevertheless the evil effects of the conflict in Europe enveloped the people of this country in its consequences. As you will recall, Macaulay, in his graphic way in the essay upon Frederick the Great, said:

In order that he might rob a neighbor whom he had promised to defend, black men fought on the coast of Coromandel and red men scalped each other by the Great Lakes of North America.

When Washington assumed the responsibilities as administrator of this Government, he immediately set about to change that condition of affairs; to wit, to separate the European system from the American system, to withdraw our people from her broils, to individualize the American Nation, and to divorce us from the quarrels and turmoils of European life. This was peculiarly and distinctly a policy originating with the Father of our Country. If there is any one thing in his entire career, marvelous as it was, which can be said to be distinctly his, it is the foreign policy which characterized his administration. His idea almost alone in the first instance was that we never could become a nation with a national mind, a national purpose, and national ideals, until we divorced ourselves from the European system. He entertained this view before he became President. I venture to recall to your minds a letter which he wrote, prior to the presidency, to Sir Edward Newenham, in which he says:

I hope the United States of America will be able to keep disengaged from the labyrinth of European politics and wars. * * * It should be the policy of the United States to administer to their wants without being engaged in their quarrels.

In 1791 he addressed a letter to Mr. Morris, in which he said:

I trust we shall never so far lose sight of our own interest and happiness as to become unnecessarily a party to these political disputes. Our local situation enables us to maintain that state with respect to them which otherwise could not, perhaps, be preserved by human wisdom.

The author from whom I quote, Senator Lodge, commenting upon this, says:

The world was told that a new power had come into being, which meant to hold aloof from Europe, and which took no interest in the balance of power or the fate of dynasties, but looked only to the welfare of its own people and to the conquest and mastery of a continent as its allotted tasks. The policy declared by the proclamation was purely American in its conception, and severed the colonial tradition at a stroke.

I digress to say I wish every boy and girl over the age of fifteen years could be induced to read the brilliant story of Washington as it is found in those two volumes. If they were not better Americans, with higher ideals, after they had read it, nothing could make them so.

Again, in a letter to Patrick Henry, dated later, he says:

I can most religiously aver that I have no wish that is incompatible with the dignity, happiness, and true interest of the people of this country. My ardent desire is, and my aim has been, so far as dependent on the executive department, to comply strictly with all our engagements, foreign and domestic, but to keep the United States free from any political connections with every other country, to see it independent of all, and under the influence of none. In a word, I want an American character, that the powers of Europe may be convinced that we act for ourselves.

Pursuing this thought and this great principle throughout his administration until he had fairly established it as a part of our foreign policy—the initiatory step of the same—he referred particularly to it in his Farewell Address. I shall detain the Senate by reading a single paragraph only. This was the conclusion of Washington after years of observation, after the most pointed experience, after eight years of administration of public affairs, and with as wide a vision and with as far-seeing a vision as ever accompanied a human mind upon this mundane sphere:

Why quit our own to stand upon foreign ground? Why, by inter-weaving our destiny with that of any part of Eur- by inter-weaving our destiny with that of any part of Europe, entangle our peace and prosperity in the toils of European ambition, rivalship, interest, humor, or caprice?

Are there people in this day who believe that Europe now and in the future shall be free of selfishness, or rivalship, of humor, of ambition, of caprice? If not, are we not undertaking the task against which the Father of our Country warned when he bade farewell to public service? "Why quit our own to stand upon foreign ground?" And yet in this proposed league of nations, in the very beginning, we are advised of an executive council which shall dominate and control its action, three members of which are Europeans, one member Asiatic, and one American.

If a controversy ever arises in which there is a conflict between the European system and the American system, or if a conflict ever arises in which their interests, their humor, their caprice, and their selfishness shall attempt to dominate the situation, shall we not have indeed quit our own to stand upon foreign ground?

Why should we interweave our destiny with the European destiny? Are we not interweaving our future and our destiny with European powers when we join a league of nations the constitution of which gives a majority vote in every single instance in which the league can ever be called into action to European powers?

Does the ex-President mean to say to an intelligent and thinking people that this league which thus grants this power of European governments is not interweaving our destiny with European destiny? Does he assume to say that that is not a departure from the plain terms of Washington's Farewell Address?

I repeat what I said upon the floor of the Senate a few weeks ago. It may be that the people of America want to do this; it may be that they think their future happiness and tranquility necessitates their doing it, but I inveigh against the misleading statement that we do not propose to do it by this league of nations. Let us be candid with those upon whom must rest the future burdens and obligations and not undertake to advise them that that is not going to happen which must necessarily and inevitably happen.

Washington succeeded in establishing the policy that we should not interfere in European affairs. It would have served no good purpose and would not have been beneficial to the American people in the least had we simply remained aloof from European affairs but had permitted Europe to transfer her system to the American Continent. Therefore, the Monroe doctrine. It was designed to support the policy of Washington. He had warned against the danger of entering Europe—the Monroe doctrine declared that Europe should not enter America. Permit me to say that one of these can not stand, in my judgment, without the support of the other. It is an inevitable result of Washington's teaching that the Monroe doctrine should exist. Indeed, such men as Mr. Coudert, the great lawyer, say that Washington's policy incorporated and included the Monroe doctrine; that Monroe's statement was simply an exemplification and application of the principle.

So, sir, in order that we might become a nation free from European broils and cease forever to have to do with European affairs, the

Washington policy and the Monroe doctrine were announced and have ever since been maintained. The great question now is, are they policies which we should still maintain; are they in all essential particulars still indispensable to our well-being as a people and to our strength and permanency as a nation? The present war has drawn us to Europe, but only temporarily. The question shall we enter European affairs permanently and shall we invite Europe, with her systems of government, some more pernicious than in the days of Washington, to America. We had a temporary alliance with France when Washington became President, but he fought against the making of these alliances permanent. That is the question here.

What is the Monroe doctrine? I apologize to the Senate for going into that question. I do so more for others than my colleagues, but I will be brief. Before the exigencies arising out of conditions connected with a defense of this league it would not have been necessary to discuss it. All understood it alike. The Monroe doctrine is simply the principle of self-defense applied to a people, and the principle of self-defense can not be the subject of arbitration or of enforcement by any one other than that one who is to claim and enforce the principle of self-defense.

The ex-President said the Monroe doctrine is covered and extended to the world. What was the condition before Monroe announced it? The world was one. Monroe determined to separate it and divide it, and that was the very object of it. It was a distinct announcement that the European system could not be transferred to America. The rest was simply detail. It was the division of two systems; it was the political partition of two continents. Monroe and Jefferson never would have contemplated for a moment sharing the enforcement of the Monroe doctrine with any nation of Europe. We would not even join with England in announcing it.

May I read here in connection with my remarks a statement by ex-Senator Root upon this particular feature? Before I do that, however, I desire to call attention to the language of Thomas Jefferson. It precedes the remark which I was about to make. This letter of Jefferson states as clearly as can be stated the prime object of the announcement of this doctrine:

The question presented by the letters you have sent me

is the most momentous which has ever been offered to my contemplation since that of independence.

Why does the Sage of Monticello rank the Monroe doctrine next to the Declaration of Independence? Because he believed as that genius of constructive government, Hamilton, believed, and Washington believed, that we could not maintain our independence without the Monroe doctrine. He believed that it was an indispensable pillar to our national independence, and second only to it in the catalogue of responsibilities and duties and obligations which rested upon us:

That made us a nation.

This sets our compass and points the course which we are to steer through the ocean of time opening on us. And never could we embark upon it under circumstances more auspicious. Our first and fundamental maxim should be never to entangle ourselves in the broils of Europe;

The Washington policy—

our second never to suffer Europe to intermeddle with cis-Atlantic affairs.

Yet the ex-President says notwithstanding this we carry out this discrimination and distinction between European affairs and American affairs when we permit the two systems to be united, to be organized and administered by a common authority. He declares that although we do entangle ourselves in the broils of Europe, although we do suffer Europe to intermeddle with cis-Atlantic affairs, it is not in conflict with the Monroe doctrine.

I now call your attention to the statement of Senator Root upon the proposition advanced by the ex-President—of sharing with other nations responsibility in enforcing this doctrine. Mr. Root says:

Since the Monroe doctrine is a declaration based upon this Nation's right of self-protection, it can not be transmuted into a joint or common declaration by American States or any number of them.

We could not even share the responsibility and the execution of the Monroe doctrine with our Commonwealths here upon the Western Continent. It is personal; it is individual; it is the law of self-defense. It belongs to us, and we alone must determine when it shall be enforced or when it shall not apply. It is the same rule and principle which Australia invokes, and correctly invokes, with reference to the German islands near Australia. It is the same principle which Japan sought to have established in the Orient. It is the principle of self-defense and not of common defense, or defense by common authority invoked and sustained by the joint act of many nations.

Yet we are solemnly advised that although we should share it with all the Governments of Europe and Asia and all the tribes of the different races which may in the future be organized into some form of government, it is still the doctrine of self-defense which Jefferson and Monroe announced and which Mr. Root so clearly explained.

I read another paragraph from Mr. Root's speech, which leaves nothing further to be said both as to meaning and the worth of this policy:

The familiar paragraphs of Washington's Farewell Address upon this subject were not rhetoric. They were intensely practical rules of conduct for the future guidance of the country:

"Europe has a set of primary interests which to us have none, or a very remote, relation. Hence, she must be engaged in frequent controversies, the causes of which are essentially foreign to our concerns. Hence, therefore, it must be unwise in us to implicate ourselves, by artificial ties, in the ordinary vicissitudes of her politics, or the ordinary combinations and collisions of her friendships or enmities. Our detached and distant situation invites and enables us to pursue a different course."

It was the same instinct which led Jefferson, in the letter to Monroe already quoted, to say:

"Our first and fundamental maxim should be, never to entangle ourselves in the broils of Europe; our second, never to suffer Europe to intermeddle with cisatlantic affairs."

The concurrence of Washington and Hamilton and Jefferson in the declaration of this principle of action entitles it to great respect. * * * Separation of influences as absolute and complete as possible was the remedy which the wisest of Americans agreed upon. It was one of the primary purposes of Monroe's declaration to insist upon this separation, and to accomplish it he drew the line at the water's edge. The problem of national protection in the distant future is one not to be solved by the first impressions of the casual observer, but only by profound study of the forces which, in the long life of nations, work out results. In this case the results of such a study by the best men of the formative period of the United States are supported by the instincts of the American democracy holding steadily in one direction for almost a century. The problem has not changed essentially. If the declaration of Monroe was right when the message was sent, it is right now.

We come now to the constitution of the proposed league of nations, which has been submitted to us. I shall not undertake to go into details; indeed, time would not permit to take up the many different phases which this constitution presents for consideration. I want only to call attention to some features of it bearing upon this particular subject matter— that is, the effect it has upon these two great policies.

The mere reading of the constitution of the

league will convince any reasonable mind, any unprejudiced mind, that if put into effect the policy of Washington and the policy of Monroe must depart. The propositions are irreconcilable and can not exist together. In the first place, the league provides for an organiation composed principally of five great nations, three of them European, one Asiatic, and one American. Every policy determined upon by the league and every movement made by it could be, and might be, controlled solely by European powers, whether the matter dealt with had reference to America or Europe. The league nowhere distinguishes or discriminates between European and American affairs. It functions in one continent the same as another. It compounds all three continents into a single unit, so far as the operations of the league are concerned. The league interferes in European affairs and in American affairs upon the same grounds and for the same reasons. If the territorial integrity of any member of the league is threatened or involved, whether that territory be in America or Europe, the league deals with the subject. If it becomes necessary for the league to act through economic pressure, or finally through military power, although the procedure may be voted by Eu-

ropean powers alone, it may exert that pressure
in America the same as in Europe. The very
object and purpose of the league is to eliminate
all differences between Europe and America
and place all in a common liability to be governed and controlled by a common authority.
If the United States, for instance, should disregard its covenants, as provided in the league,
it would be deemed to have committed an act
of war against all other members of the league;
and under one solemn obligation and agreement we would have authorized the European
powers to wage war against us and upon the
American Continent. And yet men deliberately and blandly state to the American people
that this league constitution preserves the
Monroe doctrine and the doctrine given us by
Washington.

I read from article 10 as an illustration:

The high contracting parties shall undertake to respect
and preserve as against external aggression the territorial
existence and existing political independence of all States
members of the league.

Take for illustration one of our own associates and allies. England has possessions in
three continents. As has been said, the sun
never sets upon her possessions. They dot

every sea and are found in every land. She today holds possession of one-fifth of the habita-
ble globe, and we in article 10 guarantee the
integrity of her possessions in the three continents of the earth.

So, Mr. President, the first obligation which
we assume is to protect the territorial integrity
of the British Empire. That takes us into
every part of the civilized world. That is the
most radical departure from the Washington
policy. I will come to the Monroe policy in a
minute. Now, how are we to determine that?

In case of any such aggression or in case of any threat or
danger of such aggression the executive council shall advise upon the means by which the obligation shall be
fulfilled.

Does that mean what it says, and is it to
be executed in accordance with its plain terms?
If the territorial integrity of any part of the
British Empire shall be threatened not the
Congress of the United States, not the
people of the United States, not the Government of the United States determines what
shall be done, but the executive council of
which the American people have one member.
We, if we mean what we say in this constitution, are pledging ourselves, our honor, our
sacred lives, to the preservation of the territor-

ial possessions the world over and not leaving it to the judgment and sense of the American people but to the diplomats of Europe.

That is the duty devolving upon us by virtue of the league, to enter European affairs. What would be the duty and the obligation of England, of France, of Italy, and of Japan to the other member should a disturbance arise upon the Western Continent? Suppose some threat of danger to the Republic should come from Mexico or from Mexico and its allies. We are not even consulted as to whether we shall call in help, but the duty devolves upon the council, in its initiative capacity, to at once assume jurisdiction of it and to proceed to the American continent to determine what its duties shall be with reference to American affairs. This league operates upon the Western Continent with the same jurisdiction and power and the same utter disregard of which continent it is upon as it does in the European Continent. Does anybody deny that proposition?

Let us take a homely illustration; perhaps it may better illustrate the argument. A great many years ago a man by the name of Europe opened a farm. He begins the tillage of his great farm, but turmoil, strife, and dissension arise among his tenants. Finally a dissatisfied

European by the name, we will call him, America, determines to leave these turmoils on the European farm to go into the forest, open a clearing, and establish a new farm. He says, "I shall go where I can worship God according to the dictates of my own conscience. I shall go where I can set up a new system of farming." He goes into the wilderness and sacrifices and finally establishes a farm of his own. After he has established it he declares, after reflection, "I am afraid those Europeans will come here and cause me the same disturbance and trouble and establish the same kind of a system which we had in Europe; so I will establish a partition fence." He does establish a partition fence. When he has finished the fence he says, "I will neither go to your farm nor shall you come to mine; I have had some experience with you, and I do not want to try it again." So he builds an insurmountable wall or fence between his neighbor Europe and himself. It stands for a hundred years. People sit about and discuss it, and pass many eulogies, declaring over and over again that it was one of the wisest things that a farmer ever did. But suddenly a new inspiration dawns, and it is thought that it would be a good idea to tear down the wall or fence and to commingle and intermingle the systems; to join one farm to another and have one superintendent. It is said to the farmer America, "Let us tear down this fence." He replies in surprise and consternation, "I built it for a purpose." "Well," it is contended by the idealist, "we think it is better to tear it down." At this time there rises up a man by the name of William Howard. He says to farmer America, "Let us tear down this wall fence of yours. It must be done right away. Anyone who opposes can not be trusted overnight." The farmer says, "I do not think it would be well." "But," William Howard replies, "it is just the same after it is torn down as it is when it is standing up. We are going to put a fence around both farms, and that will be the same as a fence between the farms." William Howard further says, "Let us go into partnership with your neighbor Europe." America says, "I do not want any partnership. I came here to get away from that very thing." William Howard urges, with a spirit of unselfishness and good naturedly, "It is just the same without a partnership at it is with it. Let us transmute or combine these two systems and make them one." "But," farmer America says, "I came to this country to get away from that system. I do not want one system; I want two systems. I do not like your system of farming." William Howard replies, "One system is just the same as two systems." He declares, furthermore, "I know something about this; I ran this farm for four years myself [laughter]; I know how to run it; and I declare to you that the best thing for you to do is to tear down your wall fence, to unite your two systems, and make one farm out of it and one common overseer." He further, by way of a profound argument, casually remarks, "I had such remarkable success while I was running this farm and received such universal commendation upon my work after it was over, having received the approval of two tenants out of forty-eight, that I am sure I can run both farms, at least, I am anxious to try." [Laughter.]

Some of us declare that this proposition tears down the farmer's fence. We say furthermore that we do not want two farms made into one. If you want to do so, all right, go ahead; but let us make no mistake about what we are doing. Let us not try to fool ourselves or anyone else.

What do other countries think about it, Mr. President? I should like to call in outside witnesses, notwithstanding the very profound respect that I have for the ex-President. The English press, we are informed in so far as it has commented upon this subject at all, has regarded it as an abrogation of the Monroe doctrine. Mr. Lloyd-George said in the very beginning of these conferences that Great Britain could concede much to the United States if, as the result, they were to draw the United States out of her isolation and away from her traditional foreign policies. Japan has practically announced semiofficially that it is the abolishment of the Monroe doctrine. The Brazilian Minister at The Hague has announced that it is the end of the Monroe doctrine. Why leave it in doubt? Do you Senators, or those who are in favor of the league of nations, want to destroy the Monroe doctrine? If you do not, why leave it in doubt? Why leave it to the construction of European diplomats sitting behind closed doors? By the insertion of three lines in this constitution you can place it beyond peradventure, beyond contention or cavil. The question which I submit now is, if you are unwilling to do this, is it not proof conclusive that you intend to destroy the policy and wipe out this long-standing doctrine?

Let us go to another feature of this league.

I am not here today to criticize in any way, either directly or by inference, the great English nation or the great English people. They are among, not excepting our own, the most powerful and admirable people upon the globe. Every man must pay his profound respect to their genius and to their capacity for Government and for mastery of great problems. But when we come to deal with England, we must deal with her intelligently and with a due regard for our own interests and our own rights, for one of the distinguishing characteristics of that proud nation is that England should always look after England's interests. I admire her for doing so.

Her national spirit never fails her. The talents and genius of her statesmen never betray her. She has signed many treaties which have been worthless in the hour of peril. She has entered into many leagues and combinations which have dissolved, but her proud national spirit never forsakes her. Ultimately she relies upon this instead of treaties and leagues. She has passed through many a crisis, she has seen dark hours; but in every crisis, however severe, and in the darkest hour every Englishman is expected to do his duty and does it. I admire her for her national spirit, for her vigilance in guarding the interests of the Empire.

This constitution of the league of nations is the greatest triumph for English diplomacy in three centuries of English diplomatic life. This constitution, in the first place, is lifted almost bodily, as you will see if you will compare the two, from the constitution proposed in January by Gen. Smuts. There is not an organic, a vital principle incorporated in this constitution that is not found in Gen. Smuts's constitution. As is known to all, Gen. Smuts, a South African, is one of the most remarkable men under the English rule today. That you may not think I am stating it strongly, let me read a word from the London Times on the second day after this constitution was adapted:

The project, if not the same as that outlined by Gen. Smuts, is like it as its brother. * * * It is a cause for legitimate pride to recognize in the covenant so much of the work of Englishmen. * * * It is again a source of legitimate pride to Englishmen that article 19 in the covenant might almost be taken as an exposition of the principles animating the relations of Great Britain with India and the dominions.

Listen to this language—

That the dominions are in this document recognized as nations before the world is also a fact of profound significance in the history of these relations.

The gentleman who wrote that editorial had not acquired the capacity of using language to conceal his thoughts; he labored under the disadvantage of having to use language to convey his thoughts. The fact that the dominions of Great Britain and her colonies are recognized as the nations is a matter of "profound significance." Yes; when they finally settle down to business England will have one vote, Canada one vote, New Zealand one vote, Australia one vote, and South Africa one vote, whilst the American Nation, brought into being by our fathers at so much cost of blood and treasure and preserved through the century by the vigilance and sacrifice of our forebears, this Nation with all her wealth and resources will have one vote. In both the executive council and the delegate body the same proportion obtains, and those two bodies direct, dominate, and mark out the policy of this entire program, whatever it is to be, under the league. A matter of "profound significance!"

I ask you who are in favor of this league, are you willing to give to any nation five votes against our one? Do you presume that the questions of interest, of ambition, of selfishness, of caprice, of humor will not arise in the future? Have they not already, in a proper way, but none the less in an unmistakable way, made their appearance since the armistice was signed? Are we not already advised that we must use the same intelligence, the same foresight, the same prevision, and the same patriotism that our fathers used against the inherent, the inevitable selfishness of all nations? Yet we are seriously proposing that we shall join a league whose constitutional powers shall determine—what? Shall determine policies, politic and economic, upon the two continents and shall give to our greatest commercial rival five votes to our one.

I have called attention to some of the obligations which we assume. Let me repeat a single statement. You have now observed the number of votes in the executive council, but that is not all. There are Italy and Japan associated with England, and more nearly like her in their systems and in their policies than they are like the United States. There are already treaties between those nations and England, which Mr. Balfour frankly says are not to be abrogated; in other words, we are in the very beginning put up not only against this extraordinary vote by one nation but we have the disadvantage of contending against a system, which system covers other nations as well as that of Great Britain.

We all want friendship and respect and future amicable relations between Great Britain and this country. That also was Washington's wish; that was Jefferson's wish; that was also Lincoln's wish; but never for a moment did they surrender any power or any authority or compromise their capacity in any way to take care of the situation in case there should not be an agreement between the two powers.

What has England given up in this league of nations? What has she surrendered? Will some one advise me? Did she surrender the freedom of the seas? That was pushed aside at the first meetings of the conference as not subject to its jurisdiction. Has she surrendered her claim for the largest navy? What has she surrendered?

On the other hand, we have surrendered the traditional foreign policy of this country, established for one hundred years; and we have gone behind these powers and placed at their disposal our finances, our man power, and our full capacity to guarantee the integrity of their possessions all over the globe. Is it an even balance, is it an equitable, is it an honest arrangement between these great powers and the United States?

I come now to another feature, which to me is even more interesting, more menacing, than those over which we have passed. Conceal it as you may, disguise it as some will attempt to do, this is the first step in internationalism and the first distinct effort to sterilize nationalism. This is a recognized fact, tacitly admitted by all who support it and expressly admitted by many, that the national State has broken down and that we must now depend upon the international State and international power in order to preserve our interests and our civilization. The national State can no longer serve the cause of civilization, and therefore we must resort to the international State. That is disclosed in every line and paragraph of this instrument. It begins with the preamble and ends with the last article—a recognition that internationalism must take the place of nationalism.

May I call attention to a statement from perhaps the most famous internationalist now living. I read from a book entitled "The Bolsheviki and World Peace," by Trotzky. He says:

The present war is at bottom a revolt of the forces of production against the political form of nation and state. It means the collapse of the national State as an independent economic unit.

In another paragraph:

The war proclaims the downfall of the national state. * * * We Russian Socialists stand firmly on the ground of internationalism. * * * The German social democracy was to us not only *a* party of the international —it was *the* party par excellence.

Again, he declares:

The present war signalizes the collapse of the national states.

He proceeds to argue that the only thing which can take the place of the national state is internationalism, to internationalize our governments, internationalize our power, internationalize production, internationalize our economic capacity, and become an international state the world over. That is at the bottom of this entire procedure, whether consciously or unconsciously, upon the part of those who are advocating it. It will be the fruit of this effort if it succeeds—the dead sea fruit for the common people everywhere. It is a distinct announcement that the intense nationalism of Washington, the intense nationalism of Lincoln, can no longer serve the cause of the American people, and that we must internationalize and place the sovereign powers of this Government to make war and control our economic forces in an international tribunal.

A few days ago one of the boldest and most brilliant internationalists of this country—a man, no doubt, who believes in it as firmly as I believe in nationalism—wrote this paragraph:

The death of Col. Roosevelt was a shock, I think, to everybody who loves life. No man ever lived who had more fun in 61 years; and yet his death, with that last frantic reiteration of Americanism and nothing but Americanism, fresh from his pen, was like a symbol of the progress of life. The boyish magnetism is all gone out of those words. They die in the dawn of revolutionary internationalism.

I sometimes wonder, Can it be true? Are we, indeed, yielding our Americanism before the onrushing tide of revolutionary internationalism? Did the death of this undaunted advocate of American nationalism mark an epoch in the fearful, damnable, downward trend?

Yes, this many-sided man touched life at every point, and sometimes seemed inconsistent; but there was one supreme passion which gave simplicity and singleness of purpose to all he said or did—his abounding Americanism. In this era of national infidelity let us be deeply grateful for this. Though he had erred a thousand times, and grievously erred, we would still pay sincere tribute to his memory for holding aloft at all times, and especially in the world's greatest turmoil, the banner of the true faith. Huntsmen, plainsmen, author, political leader, governor, Vice President, President, and ex-President, this was always the directing and dominating theme. Even in his full, rich life, replete with noble deeds and brilliant achievements, it runs like a golden thread through all of the bewildering activities of his wide-ranging genius. It gave consistency to every change of view and justified what sometimes seemed his merciless intolerance. When the final estimate is placed upon his career, and all his services to his fellows are weighed and judged, his embodiment of the national spirit, his vigilant defense of our national integrity, his exemplification of our national ideals will distinguish him, as says in effect this internationalist, from all the men of his day and generation.

I am not a pessimist. I find neither solace nor guidance in the doleful doctrine. But who will gainsay that we have reached a supreme hour in the history of the Republic he loved? There is not a Government in existence today but feels the strain of those inscrutable forces which are working their wilful way through all the established institutions of men. Church and creed, ancient governments and new, despotic and liberal, order and law, at this time stand under challenge. Hunger and disease, business anxiety, and industrial unrest threaten to demobilize the moral forces of organized society. In all of this turmoil and strife, in all this chaos of despair and hope, there is much that is good if it can be brought under direction and subordinated to the sway of reason. At the bottom of it all there is the infinite longing of oppressed humanity seeking in madness to be rid of oppression and to escape from these centuries of injustice. How shall we help to bring order out of chaos? Shall we do so by becoming less or more American? Shall we entangle and embarrass the efforts of a powerful and independent people, or shall we leave them in every emergency and in every crisis to do in that particular hour and in that supreme moment what the conscience and wisdom of an untrammeled and liberty-loving people shall decide as wise and just? Or shall we yoke our deliberations to forces we can not control and leave our people to the mercy of powers which may be wholly at variance with our conception of duty? I may be willing to help my neighbor, though he be improvident or unfortunate, but I do not necessarily want him for a business partner. I may be willing to give liberally of my means, of my council and advice, even of my strength or blood, to protect his family from attack or injustice, but I do not want him placed in a position where he may decide for me when and how I shall act or to what extent I shall make sacrifice. I do not want this Republic, its intelligence, and its patriotism, its free people and its institutions to go into partnership with and to give control of the partnership to those, many of whom have no conception of our civilization and no true insight into our destiny. What we want is what Roosevelt taught and urged—a free, untrammeled Nation, imbued anew and inspired again with the national spirit. Not isolation but freedom to do as our own people think wise and just; not isolation but simply the unembarrassed and unentangled freedom of a great Nation to determine for itself and in its own way where duty lies and where wisdom calls. There is not a supreme council possible of creation or conceivable equal in wisdom, in conscience, and humanitarianism to the wisdom and conscience and humanitarianism of the hundred million free and independent liberty-loving souls to whom the living God has intrusted the keeping of this Nation. The moment this Republic comes to any other conclusion it has forfeited its right to live as an independent and self-respecting Republic.

It was not, one likes to believe, a mere incident, but a significant though strangely arranged fact that the last message to the American people from the illustrious dead who, the internationalists tell us, was the last of the great Americans, should have been upon this particular subject. I believe it was the night of his death that this message which I shall now read to you was read at a public meeting to which he had been invited but was unable to attend:

Any man who says he is an American but something else also isn't an American at all. We have room for but one flag, the American flag. * * * We have room for but one language, and that is the English language; for we intend to see that the crucible turns our people out as Americans, of American nationality, and not as dwellers in a polyglot boarding house; and we have room for but one soul loyalty to the American people.

Let us inscribe this upon our banner and hang it upon the outer wall. In all the vicissitudes of our national life, in all the duties which may come to us as a people, in all the future, filled, as it will be, with profound and perplexing problems, let us cling uncompromisingly to this holy creed. In these times, when ancient faiths are disappearing and governments are crumbling, when institutions are yielding to the tread of the mad hosts of disorder, let us take our stand on the side of orderly liberty, on the side of constitutional government. Let us range ourselves along with Washington and Jefferson and Jackson and Lincoln and Roosevelt. Let us be true to ourselves; and, whatever the obligations of the future, we can not then be false to others.

IX

THE LEAGUE OF NATIONS
November 19, 1919

(The Senate had under final consideration the resolution of ratification of the peace treaty.)

Mr. President, after Mr. Lincoln had been elected President before he assumed the duties of the office and at a time when all indications were to the effect that we would soon be in the midst of civil strife, a friend from the city of Washington wrote him for instructions. Mr. Lincoln wrote back in a single line, "Entertain no compromise; have none of it." That states the position I occupy at this time and which I have, in an humble way, occupied from the first contention in regard to this proposal.

My objections to the league have not been met by the reservations. I desire to state wherein my objections have not been met. Let us see what our attitude will be toward Europe and what our position will be with reference to the other nations of the world after we shall have entered the league with the present reservations written therein. With all due respect to those who think that they have accomplished a different thing and challenging no man's intellectual integrity or patriotism, I do not believe the reservations have met the fundamental propositions which are involved in this contest.

When the league shall have been formed, we shall be a member of what is known as the council of the league. Our accredited representative will sit in judgment with the accredited representatives of the other members of the league to pass upon the concerns not only of our country but of all Europe and all Asia and the entire world. Our accredited representatives will be members of the assembly. They will sit there to represent the judgment of these 110,000,000 of people, just as we are accredited here to represent our constituencies. We can not send our representatives to sit in council with the representatives of the other great nations of the world with mental reservations as to what we shall do in case their judgment shall not be satisfactory to us. If we go to the council or to the assembly with any other purpose than that of complying in good faith and in absolute integrity with all upon which the council or the assembly may pass, we shall soon return to our country with our self-respect forfeited and the public opinion of the world condemnatory.

Why need you gentlemen across the aisle worry about a reservation here or there, when we are sitting in the council and in the assembly and bound by every obligation in morals, which the President said was supreme above that of law, to comply with the judgment which our representative and the other representatives finally form? Shall we go there, to sit in judgment, and in case that judgment works for peace join with our allies, but in case it works for war withdraw our cooperation? How long would we stand as we now stand, a great Republic commanding the respect and holding the leadership of the world, if we should adopt any such course?

So, sir, we not only sit in the council and in the assembly with our accredited representatives, but bear in mind that article 11 is untouched by any reservation which has been offered here; and with article 11 untouched, and its integrity complete, article 10 is perfectly superfluous. If any war or threat of war shall be a matter of consideration for the league, and the league shall take such action as it deems wise to deal with it, what is the necessity of article 10? Will not external aggression be regarded as a war or threat of war? If the political independence of some nation in Europe is assailed will it be regarded as a war or threat of war? Is there anything in article 10 that is not completely covered by article 11?

It remains complete, and with our representatives sitting in the council and the assembly, and with article 11 complete, and with the assembly and the council having jurisdiction of all matters touching the peace of the world, what more do you need to bind the United States if you assume that the United States is a Nation of honor?

We have said that we would not send our troops abroad without the consent of Congress. Pass by now for a moment the legal proposition. If we create executive functions, the Executive will perform those functions without the authority of Congress. Pass that question by and go to the other question. Our members of the council are there. Our members of the assembly are there. Article 11 is complete, and it authorizes the league, a member of which is our representative, to deal with matters of peace and war, and the league through its council and its assembly deals with the matter, and our accredited representative joins with the others in deciding upon a certain course,

which involves a question of sending troops.
What will the Congress of the United States
do? What right will it have left, except the
bare technical right to refuse, which as a moral
proposition it will not dare to exercise? Have
we not been told day by day for the last nine
months that the Senate of the United States,
a coordinate part of the treaty-making power,
should accept this league as it was written because the wise men sitting at Versailles had
so written it, and has not every possible influence and every source of power in public opinion been organized and directed against the
Senate to compel it to do that thing? How
much stronger will be the moral compulsion
upon the Congress of the United States when
we ourselves have indorsed the proposition of
sending our accredited representatives there
to vote for us?

Ah, but you say that there must be unanimous consent, and that there is vast protection
in unanimous consent.

I do not wish to speak disparagingly; but
has not every division and dismemberment of
every nation which has suffered dismemberment taken place by unanimous consent for the
last three hundred years? Did not Prussia
and Austria and Russia by unanimous consent

divide Poland? Did not the United States and Great Britain and Japan and Italy and France divide China, and give Shantung to Japan? Was that not a unanimous decision? Close the doors upon the diplomats of Europe, let them sit in secret, give them the material to trade on, and there always will be unanimous consent.

How did Japan get unanimous consent? I want to say here, in my parting words upon this proposition, that I have no doubt the outrage upon China was quite as distasteful to the President of the United States as it is to me. But Japan said: "I will not sign your treaty unless you turn over to me Shantung, to be turned back at my discretion," and you know how Japan's discretion operates with reference to such things. And so, when we are in the league, and our accredited representatives are sitting at Geneva, and a question of great moment arises, Japan, or Russia, or Germany, or Great Britain will say, "Unless this matter is adjusted in this way I will depart from your league." It is the same thing, operating in the same way, only under a different date and under a little different circumstances.

If you have enough territory, if you have enough material, if you have enough subject peoples to trade upon and divide, there will be no difficulty about unanimous consent.

Do our Democratic friends ever expect any man to sit as a member of the council or as a member of the assembly equal in intellectual power and in standing before the world with that of our representative at Versailles? Do you expect a man to sit in the council who will have made more pledges, and I shall assume made them in sincerity, for self-determination and for the rights of small peoples, than had been made by our accredited representative? And yet, what became of it? The unanimous consent was obtained nevertheless.

But take another view of it. We are sending to the council one man. That one man represents 110,000,000 people.

Here, sitting in the Senate, we have two from every State in the Union, and over in the other House we have Representatives in accordance with population, and the responsibility is spread out in accordance with our obligations to our constituency. But now we are transferring to one man the stupendous power of representing the sentiment and convictions of 110,000,000 people in tremendous questions which may involve the peace or may involve the war of the world.

However you view the question of unanimous consent, it does not protect us.

What is the result of all this? We are in the midst of all of the affairs of Europe. We have entangled ourselves with all European concerns. We have joined in alliance with all the European nations which have thus far joined the league, and all nations which may be admitted to the league. We are sitting there dabbling in their affairs and intermeddling in their concerns. In other words — and this comes to the question which is fundamental with me—we have forfeited and surrendered, once and for all, the great policy of "no entangling alliances" upon which the strength of this Republic has been founded for one hundred and fifty years.

My friends of reservations, tell me where is the reservation in these articles which protects us against entangling alliances with Europe?

Those who are differing over reservations, tell me what one of them protects the doctrine laid down by the Father of our Country. That fundamental proposition is surrendered, and we are a part of the European turmoils and conflicts from the time we enter this league.

Let us not underestimate that. There has never been an hour since the Venezuelan difficulty that there has not been operating in this country, fed by domestic and foreign sources, a powerful propaganda for the destruction of the doctrine of no entangling alliances.

Lloyd-George is reported to have said just a few days before the conference met at Versailles that Great Britain could give up much, and would be willing to sacrifice much, to have America withdraw from that policy. That was one of the great objects of the entire conference at Versailles, so far as the foreign representatives were concerned. Clemenceau and Lloyd-George and others like them were willing to make any reasonable sacrifice which would draw America away from her isolation and into the internal affairs and concerns of Europe. This league of nations, with or without reservations, whatever else it does or does not do, does surrender and sacrifice that policy; and once having surrendered and become a part of the European concerns, where, my friends, are you going to stop?

You have put in here a reservation upon the Monroe doctrine. I think that, in so far as language could protect the Monroe doctrine, it has been protected. But as a practical proposition, as a working proposition, tell me candidly, as men familiar with the history of your country and of other countries, do you think that you can intermeddle in European affairs and keep Europe from intermeddling in your affairs?

When Mr. Monroe wrote to Jefferson, he asked him his view upon the Monroe doctrine, and Mr. Jefferson said, in substance, our first and primary obligation should be never to interfere in European affairs; and, secondly, never permit Europe to interfere in our affairs.

He understood, as every wise and practical man understands, that if we intermeddle in her affairs, if we help to adjust her conditions, inevitably and remorselessly Europe then will be carried into our affairs, in spite of anything you can write upon paper.

We can not protect the Monroe doctrine unless we protect the basic principle upon which it rests, and that is the Washington policy. I do not care how earnestly you may endeavor to do so, as a practical working proposition, your league will come to the United States. Will you permit me to digress long enough to read a paragraph from a great French editor upon this particular phase of the matter, Mr. Stephen Lausanne, editor of *Le Matin,* of Paris:

When the executive council of the league of nations fixes "the reasonable limits of the armament of Peru"; when it shall demand information concerning the naval program of Brazil; when it shall tell Argentina what shall be the measure of the "contribution to the armed forces to protect the signatures of the social covenant"; when it shall demand the immediate registration of the treaty between the United States and Canada at the seat of the league, it will control, whether it will or no, the destines of America. And when the American States shall be obliged to take a hand in every war or menace of war in Europe (art. 11), they will necessarily fall afoul of the fundamental principle laid down by Monroe, which was that Americans should never take part in a European war.

If the league takes in the world, then Europe must mix in the affairs of America; if only Europe is included, then America will violate of necessity her own doctrine by intermixing in the affairs of Europe.

If the league includes the affairs of the world, does it not include the affairs of all the world? Is there any limitation of the jurisdiction of the council or of the assembly upon the question of peace or war? Does it not have now, under the reservations, the same as it had before, the power to deal with all matters of peace or war throughout the entire world? How shall you keep from meddling in the affairs of Europe or keep Europe from meddling in the affairs of America?

There is another and even a more commanding reason why I shall record my vote against this treaty. It imperils what I conceive to be the underlying, the very first principles of this Republic. It is in conflict with the right of our people to govern themselves free from all restraint, legal or moral, of foreign powers. It challenges every tenet of my political faith. If this faith were one of my own contriving, if I stood here to assert principles of government of my own evolving, I might well be charged with intolerable presumption, for we all recognize the ability of those who urge a different course. But I offer in justification of my course nothing of my own—save the deep and abiding reverence I have for those whose policies I humbly but most ardently support. I claim no merit save fidelity to American principles and devotion to American ideals as they were wrought out from time to time by those who built the Republic and as they have been extended and maintained throughout these years. In opposing the treaty I do nothing more than decline to renounce and tear out of my life the sacred traditions which through fifty years have been translated into my whole intellectual and moral being. I will not, I can not, give up my belief that America must, not alone for the happiness of her own people, but for the moral guidance and greater contentment of the world,

be permitted to live her own life. Next to the
tie which binds a man to his God is the tie
which binds a man to his country, and all
schemes, all plans, however ambitious and fascinating they seem in their proposal, but which
would embarrass or entangle and impede or
shackle her sovereign will, which would compromise her freedom of action I unhesitatingly
put behind me.

Sir, since the debate opened months ago
those of us who have stood against this proposition have been taunted many times with being little Americans. Leave us the word
American, keep that in your presumptuous im-
peachment, and no taunt can disturb us, no
gibe discompose our purposes. Call us little
Americans if you will, but leave us the consolation and the pride which the term American,
however modified, still imparts. Take away
that term and though you should coin in telling
phrase your highest eulogy we would hurl it
back as common slander. We have been ridi-
culed because, forsooth, of our limited vision.
Possibly that charge may be true. Who is
there here that can read the future? Time, and
time alone, unerring and remorseless, will give
us each our proper place in the affections of our
countrymen and in the esteem and commenda-

tion of those who are to come after us. We neither fear nor court her favor. But if our vision has been circumscribed it has at all times within its compass been clear and steady. We have sought nothing save the tranquility of our own people and the honor and independence of our own Republic. No foreign flattery, no possible world glory and power have disturbed our poise or come between us and our devotion to the traditions which have made us a people. or the policies which have made us a Nation, unselfish and commanding. If we have erred we have erred out of too much love for those things which from childhood you and we together have been taught to revere—yes, to defend even at the cost of limb and life. If we have erred it is because we have placed too high an estimate upon the wisdom of Washington and Jefferson, too exalted an opinion upon the patriotism of the sainted Lincoln. And blame us not therefore if we have, in our limited vision, seemed sometimes bitter and at all times uncompromising, for the things for which we have spoken, feebly spoken, the things which we have endeavored to defend have been the things for which your fathers and our fathers were willing to die.

Senators, even in an hour so big with expec-

fancy we should not close our eyes to the fact that democracy is something more, vastly more, than a mere form of government by which society is restrained into free and orderly life. It is a moral entity, a spiritual force as well. And these are things which live only and alone in the atmosphere of liberty. The foundation upon which democracy rests is faith in the moral instincts of the people. Its ballot boxes, the franchise, its laws, and constitutions are but the outward manifestations of the deeper and more essential thing — a continuing trust in the moral purposes of the average man and woman. When this is lost or forfeited your outward forms, however democratic in terms, are a mockery. Force may find expression through institutions democratic in structure equally with the simple and more direct processes of a single supreme ruler. These distinguishing virtues of a real republic you can not commingle with the discordant and destructive forces of the Old World and still preserve them. You can not yoke a government whose fundamental maxim is that of liberty to a government whose first law is that of force and hope to preserve the former. These things are in eternal war, and one must ultimately destroy the other. You may still keep for a time the outward form, you may still delude your-self, as others have done in the past, with appearances and symbols, but when you shall have committed this Republic to a scheme of world control based upon force, upon the combined military force of the four great nations of the world, you will have soon destroyed the atmosphere of freedom, of confidence in the self-governing capacity of the masses, in which alone a democracy may thrive. We may become one of the four dictators of the world, but we shall no longer be master of our own spirit. And what shall it profit us as a Nation if we shall go forth to the dominion of the earth and share with others the glory of world control and lose that fine sense of confidence in the people, the soul of democracy.

Look upon the scene as it is now presented. Behold the task we are to assume, and then contemplate the method by which we are to deal with this task. Is the method such as to address itself to a Government "conceived in liberty and dedicated to the proposition that all men are created equal"? When this league, this combination, is formed four great powers representing the dominant people will rule one-half of the inhabitants of the globe as subject peoples—rule by force, and we shall be a party to the rule of force. There is no other way by which you can keep people in subjection. You must either give them independence, recognize their rights as nations to live their own life and to set up their own form of government, or you must deny them these things by force. That is the scheme, the method proposed by the league. It proposes no other. We will in time become inured to its inhuman precepts and its soulless methods, strange as this doctrine now seems to a free people. If we stay with our contract, we will come in time to declare with our associates that force—force, the creed of the Prussian military oligarchy—is after all the true foundation upon which must rest all stable governments. Korea, despoiled and bleeding at every pore; India, sweltering in ignorance and burdened with inhuman taxes after more than a hundred years of dominant rule; Egypt, trapped and robbed of her birthright; Ireland, with 700 years of sacrifice for independence—this is the task, this is the atmosphere, and this is the creed in and under which we are to keep alive our belief in the moral purposes and self-governing capacity of the people, a belief without which the Republic must disintegrate and die. The maxim of liberty will soon give way to the rule of blood and iron. We have been pleading here for our Constitution. Conform this league, it has been said, to the technical terms of our charter and all will be well. But I declare to you that we must go further and conform to those sentiments and passions for justice and freedom which are essential to the existence of democracy. You must respect not territorial boundaries, not territorial integrity, but you must respect and preserve the sentiments and passions for justice and for freedom which God in his infinite wisdom has planted so deep in the human heart that no form of tyranny however brutal, no persecution however prolonged can wholly uproot and kill. Respect nationality, respect justice, respect freedom, and you may have some hope of peace, but not so if you make your standard the standard of tyrants and despots, the protection of real estate regardless of how it is obtained.

Sir, we are told that this treaty means peace. Even so, I would not pay the price. Would you purchase peace at the cost of any part of our independence? We could have had peace in 1776—the price was high, but we could have had it. James Otis, Sam Adams, Hancock, and Warren were surrounded by those who urged peace and British rule. All through that long and trying struggle, particularly when the clouds of adversity lowered upon the cause there was a cry of peace—let us have peace. We could have had peace in 1860; Lincoln was counseled by men of great influence and accredited wisdom to let our brothers—and, thank heaven, they are brothers—depart in peace. But the tender, loving Lincoln, bending under the fearful weight of impending civil war, an apostle of peace, refused to pay the price, and a reunited country will praise his name forevermore—bless it because he refused peace at the price of national honor and national integrity. Peace upon any other basis than national independence, peace purchased at the cost of any part of our national integrity, is fit only for slaves, and even when purchased at such a price it is a delusion, for it can not last.

But your treaty does not mean peace—far, very far, from it. If we are to judge the future by the past it means war. Is there any guaranty of peace other than the guaranty which comes of the control of the war-making power by the people? Yet what great rule of democracy does the treaty leave unassailed? The people in whose keeping alone you can safely lodge the power of peace or war nowhere, at no time and in no place, have any voice in this scheme for world peace. Autocracy which has bathed the world in blood for centuries reigns supreme. Democracy is everywhere excluded. This, you say, means peace.

Can you hope for peace when love of country is disregarded in your scheme, when the spirit of nationality is rejected, even scoffed at? Yet what law of that moving and mysterious force does your treaty not deny? With a ruthlessness unparalleled your treaty in a dozen instances runs counter to the divine law of nationality. Peoples who speak the same language, kneel at the same ancestral tombs, moved by the same traditions, animated by a common hope, are torn asunder, broken in pieces, divided, and parceled out to antagonistic nations. And this you call justice. This, you cry, means peace. Peoples who have dreamed of independence, struggled and been patient, sacrificed and been hopeful, peoples who were told that through this peace conference they should realize the aspirations of centuries, have again had their hopes dashed to earth. One of the most striking and commanding figures in this war, soldier and statesman, turned away from the peace table at Versailles declaring to the world, "The promise of the new life, the victory of the great humane ideals for which the peoples have shed their blood and their treasure without stint, the fulfillment of their aspirations toward a new international order and a fairer and better world are not written into the treaty." No; your treaty means injustice. It means slavery. It means war. And to all this you ask this Republic to become a party. You ask it to abandon the creed under which it has grown to power and accept the creed of autocracy, the creed of repression and force.

I turn from this scheme based upon force to another scheme, planned one hundred and forty-three years ago in old Independence Hall, in the city of Philadelphia, based upon liberty. I like it better. I have become so accustomed to believe in it that it is difficult for me to reject it out of hand. I have difficulty in subscribing to the new creed of oppression, the creed of dominant and subject peoples. I feel a reluctance to give up the belief that all men are created equal—the eternal principle in government that all governments derive their just powers from the consent of the governed. I can not get my consent to exchange the doctrine of George Washington for the doctrine of Frederick the Great translated into mendacious phrases of peace. I go back to that serene and masterful soul who pointed the way to power and glory for the new and then weak Republic, and whose teachings and admonitions even in our majesty and dominance we dare not disregard.

I know well the answer to my contention. It has been piped about of late from a thousand sources—venal sources, disloyal sources, sinister sources—that Washington's wisdom was of his day only and that his teachings are out of fashion—things long since sent to the scrap heap of history—that while he was great in character and noble in soul he was untrained in the arts of statecraft and unlearned in the science of government. The puny demagogue, the barren editor, the sterile professor now vie with each other in apologizing for the temporary and commonplace expedients which the Father of our Country felt constrained to adopt in building a republic!

What is the test of statesmanship? Is it the formation of theories, the utterance of abstract and incontrovertible truths, or is it the capacity and the power to give to a people that concrete thing called liberty, that vital and indispensable thing in human happiness called free institutions and to establish over all and above all the blessed and eternal reign of order and law?

If this be the test, where shall we find another whose name is entitled to be written beside the name of Washington? His judgment and poise in the hour of turmoil and peril, his courage and vision in times of adversity, his firm grasp of fundamental principles, his almost inspired power to penetrate the future and read there the result, the effect of policies, have never been excelled, if equalled, by any of the world's commonwealth builders. Peter the Great, William the Silent, and Cromwell the Protector, these and these alone perhaps are to be associated with his name as the builders of States and the founders of governments. But in exaltation of moral purpose, in the unselfish character of his work, in the durability of his policies, in the permanency of the institutions which he more than anyone else called into effect, his service to mankind stands out separate and apart in a class by itself. The works of these other great builders, where are they now? But the work of Washington is still the most potent influence for the advancement of civilization and the freedom of the race.

Reflect for a moment over his achievements. He led the Revolutionary Army to victory. He was the very first to suggest a union instead of a confederacy. He presided over and counseled with great wisdom the convention which framed the Constitution. He guided the Government through its first perilous years. He gave dignity and stability and honor to that which was looked upon by the world as a passing experiment, and finally, my friends, as his own peculiar and particular contribution to the happiness of his countrymen and to the cause of the Republic, he gave us his great foreign policy under which we have lived and prospered and strengthened for nearly a century and a half. This policy is the most sublime confirmation of his genius as a statesman. It was then, and it now is an indispensable part of our whole scheme of government. It is today a vital, indispensable element in our entire plan, purpose, and mission as a nation. To abandon it is nothing less than a betrayal of the American people. I say betrayal deliberately, in view of the suffering and the sacrifice which will follow in the wake of such a course.

But under the stress and strain of these extraordinary days, when strong men are being swept down by the onrushing forces of disorder and change, when the most sacred things of life, the most cherished hopes of a Christian world seem to yield to the mad forces of discontent—just such days as Washington passed through when the mobs of Paris, wild with new liberty and drunk with power, challenged the established institutions of all the world, but his steadfast soul was unshaken—under these conditions come again we are about to abandon this policy so essential to our happiness and tranquillity as a people and our stability as a Government. No leader with his commanding influence and his unquailing courage stands forth to stem the current. But what no leader can or will do experience, bitter experience, and the people of this country in whose keeping, after all, thank God, is the Republic, will ultimately do. If we abandon his leadership and teachings, we will go back. We will return to this policy. Americanism shall not, can not die. We may go back in sackcloth and ashes, but we will return to the faith of the fathers. America will live her own life. The independence of this Republic will have its defenders. Thousands have suffered and died for it, and their sons and daughters are not of the breed who will be betrayed into the hands of foreigners. The noble face of the Father of his Country, so familiar to every boy and girl, looking out from the walls of the Capitol in stern reproach, will call those who come here for public service to a reckoning. The people of our beloved country will finally speak, and we will return to the policy which we now abandon. American disenthralled and free in spite of all these things will continue her mission in the cause of peace, of freedom, and of civilization.

X

THE VERSAILLES TREATY

(Excerpt from Speech in Senate Monday, September 26, 1921.)

Mr. President, my aversion to the Versailles treaty, to principles upon which it is built, the old imperialistic policies which have brought the world into sad ruin, makes it impossible for me to ever vote for any treaty which gives even moral recognition to that instrument. That alone would prevent me from voting for this treaty.

I am not forgetful, I trust, of the times and circumstances under which the Versailles treaty was written. They were extraordinary; they were without precedent. All the suffering and passions of a terrible war, led by the intolerant spirit of triumph, were present and dominant. It was a dictated treaty, dictated by those who yet felt the agony of conflict and whose fearful hours of sacrifice, now changed to hours of victory, thought only in terms of punishment. It was too much to expect anything else. We gain nothing, therefore; indeed, we lose much by going back to criticize or assail the individuals who had to do with its making; it was a treaty born of a fiendlike struggle and also of the limitations of human nature. So let its making pass.

But three years have come and gone since the war, and we have now had time to reflect and to contemplate the future. We have escaped, I trust, to some extent the grip of the war passion and are freer to think of the things which are to come rather than upon the things which are past. We have had time not only to read this treaty and think it over, but we have had an opportunity to see its effects upon peace and civiliation. We know what it is now, and if we recognize it and strengthen it or help to maintain it, we shall not be able to plead at the bar of history the extenuating circumstances which its makers may justly plead. We see now not alone the punishment it would visit upon the Central Powers, but we see the cruel and destructive punishment it has visited and is to visit upon millions, many of whom fought by our side in the war. We know it has reduced to subjection and delivered over to exploitation subject and friendly peoples; that it has given in exchange for promises of independence and freedom dependence and spoliation. But that is not the worst. "If it were done when it is done," we could turn our backs upon the past and hope to find exculpation in doing better things in the future. But we know this treaty has in it the seeds of many wars. It hangs like a storm cloud upon the horizon. It is the incarnation of force. It recognizes neither mercy nor repentance, and discriminates not at all between the guilty and the innocent, friend or foe. Its one-time defenders now are frank to admit it. It will bring sorrow to the world again. Its basic principle is cruel, unconscionable, and remorseless imperialism. Its terms will awaken again the reckoning power of retribution—the same power which brought to a full accounting those who cast lots over Poland and who tore Alsace-Lorraine from her coveted allegiance. We know that Europe can not recover so long as this treaty exists; that economic breakdown in Europe, if not the world, awaits its execution; and that millions of men, women, and children, those now living and those yet unborn, are to be shackled, enslaved, and hungered if it remains the law of Europe. All this we know, and knowing it we not only invite the lashings of retribution, but we surrender every tenet of the American faith when we touch the cruel and maledict thing.

When the treaty was written it had incorporated in it the so-called League of Nations. I believe it correct to say the treaty proper was only accepted by Mr. Wilson because the league was attached. I have never believed, I have never supposed, he could have been induced to accept this treaty, so at variance with every principle he had advocated and all things for which he had stood, had he not believed the league in time would ameliorate its terms and humanize its conditions. In that, of course, I think he was greatly in error.

In my opinion the league, had it been effective at all, would have been but the instrument to more effectually execute the sinister mandates of the predominant instrument. Under the treaty the league would have quickly grown into an autocracy, an autocracy based upon force, the organized military force of the great powers of the world. But now, so far as we are concerned, the league has been stricken from the document. The sole badge of respectability, the sole hope of amelioration, so far as American advocates were concerned, now vanish. With the league stricken out, who is there left in America, reared under the principles of a free government, to defend the terms and conditions of this treaty? There it is, harsh, hideous, naked, dismembering friendly peoples, making possible and justifying the exploitation of vast populations, a check to progress and at war with every principle which the founders interwove into the fabric of this Republic and challenging every precept upon which the peace of the world may be built. For such a treaty I loathe to see my country even pay the respect of recognition, much less to take anything under its terms.

Some nation or people must lead in a different course from the course announced by this treaty and its policies or the human family is to sink back into hopeless barbarism. Reflect upon the situation. We see about us on every hand in the whole world around conditions difficult to describe—a world convulsed by the agonies which the follies and crimes of leaders have laid upon the people. Hate seems almost a law of life and devastation a fixed habit of the race. Science has become the prostitute of war, while the arts of statecraft are busy with schemes for pillaging helpless and subject peoples. Trade is suspended, industry is paralyzed, famine, ravenous and insatiable, gathers millions into its skeleton clutches, while unemployment spreads and discontent deepens. The malign shadows of barbarism are creeping up and over the outskirts of civilization. And this condition is due more to the policies which the political dictators of Europe have imposed upon that continent since the armistice than any other one thing. Repression, reprisal, blockades, disregard of solemn pledges, the scheming and grabbing for the natural resources of helpless peoples, the arming of Poland, the fitting out of expeditions into Russia, the fomenting of war between Greece and Turkey, and, finally, the maintenance of an insurmountable obstacle to rehabilitation in the Versailles treaty—how could Europe, how can Europe, ever recover? Is there no nation to call a halt? Is there no country to announce the gospel of tolerance and to denounce the brutal creed of force and to offer to a dying world something besides intrigue and armaments?

In this stupendous and bewildered crisis America must do her part. No true American wants to see her shirk any part of her responsibility. There are no advocates of selfishness, none so fatuous as to urge that we may be happy and prosperous while the rest of the world is plunging on in misery and want. Call it providence, call it fate, but we know that in the nexus of things there must be something of a common sharing, all but universal and inexorable in the burdens which these great catastrophies place upon the human family. It is not only written in the great book but it is written in the economic laws of nature—"Bear ye one another's burdens." We do not differ as to the duty of America, we differ only as to the manner in which she shall discharge that duty.

We say to surrender her ancient policies or give up her great maxims of liberty means not service to mankind, but means the extinction of the last great hope of civilization. America can not be of service to the cause of humanity nor true to herself, she can not show her friendship to the world nor loyalty to her own, by accepting or recognizing, much less encouraging or joining, these policies and programs which are wrecking Europe. We can not serve the cause of reconstruction or of rebuilding by encouraging or taking advantage of this vast scheme of repression and destruction. We can not be loyal either to our own or to others by abandoning the policies which have made us great and strong; by surrendering the maxims of justice and liberty, of reason and tolerance, and accepting the creed of tooth and claw—the supreme law of the jungle. Neither can we long retain our self-respect, nor the respect of others, by having our ambassadors and agents sitting about the councils and commissions of Europe like human hawks to prey with others upon the oil wealth of Mosul or of Mesopotamia, or perchance gather some moiety of trade from plundered peoples and then take wing in case the victim stirs. This Republic, the Republic of Washington and Lincoln, can not afford to pursue such a course, at once so futile and so ignominous. It is not to her interest or to the interest of the world that she do so. Undoubtedly by reason of our participation in the war and by the terms of the armistice we have the technical right to demand our portion of the spoils, but we have a higher right and a more commanding right to insist that these peoples shall not be despoiled of their wealth and left eternal paupers in the poorhouse of the world. We want trade; we want to secure trade. We have always wanted it and we have always secured it in an honorable and successful way. But the nation which can see no other way to power save through intrigue and overreaching; which knows no other source of law than that of force; which refuses to recognize there is a thing called justice, a law of right and wrong, the law by which all governments must at last be tested, can never be a strong nation, a powerful nation, regardless of the amount of its trade or of the extent of its territorial dominion. It has been said that opinions alter, manners change, creeds rise and fall, races come and go, nations dominate and depart, but the moral law remains. The Versailles treaty, in my judgment, is the most pronounced negation of that moral law which has yet been crystalized into form by the hand of man. It must in the end, after working what evil and enforcing what misery it may, also perish. I want no favor from its terms. I want no recognition of its policy.

Mr. President, one of the revolting monstrosities born of this war, the illegitimate offspring of secret diplomacy and violence, is the absurd, iniquitous belief that you can only have peace through martial means—that force, force, is the only power left on earth with which to govern men. I denounce the hideous, diabolical idea, and I insist that this Government ought to be counted against all plans, all treaties, all programs, all policies, based upon this demonical belief. Let us have an American policy. Or, if the word "American" be considered by some as provincial or distasteful

—a term of incivility—then let us have a humane policy, a Christian policy, a policy based upon justice, resting upon reason, guided by conscience, and made dominant by the mobilized moral forces of the world.

I hear them say unsafe, impractical, powerless, insecure. I assert it is the only hope— the only escape from barbarism. Properly led, properly organized by a great people like this it will win, it will dominate, it will bring order out of chaos. When Woodrow Wilson went to Europe, carrying with him a new code, he could have overthrown any ministry in Europe, so strong was public opinion, so irresistible the moral purposes of the masses. How, by what means did he secure this power? By the power of an idea, by an appeal to the better side of man's nature—a plea for liberty, a plea for justice, a plea for reason. But they closed the doors. Behind the doors intrigue and barter and surrender dominated. When the doors opened the new code had disappeared. A treaty of militarism and imperialism, oppression, and exploitation came in its stead. A treaty which Clemenceau has declared is but a continuation of the war. Public opinion fell away. The people lost hope, the liberal forces of the world became disorganized. Discontent and despair reigned throughout Europe. Democracy gave way to bolshevism. Rapine and murder and war and famine now curse the face of the whole Continent. Ruthlessness triumphed. Everything which we were told the Prussian would do if he won the war this treaty does to some one or to some people. There is not a principle of Bernhardi but may be found in this treaty. How can we compromise with it? How can we take favors of this betrayal of a race?

Be not deceived, my friends, God is not mocked. "What a man soweth, that shall he also reap"—a law which obtains with nations as with men. You know the fate that awaited the despoilers of Poland—the brand of Cain was upon the guilty nations from the hour the partition was finished. They now stand at the judgment bar of an overruling Providence, humiliated and dishonored, broken and bleeding. You know the judgment, swift and condign, as we measure the life of nations, that awaited the author of the crime of Alsace-Lorraine. The Saar Basin, upper Silesia, and Danzig, to say nothing of others, carry with them the same seeds of war, the same weird promise of retribution. You know that Shantung bodes ill to the world's peace. You know that Syria and

Mesopotamia and Egypt, after being promised freedom and independence, are now being reduced to subjection and despoiled of the wealth which is theirs. Why prolong the story? The laws of justice may be thwarted for a time, but they can not be permanently suspended. The rule of righteousness is no respecter of persons or of peoples. Dare we longer connive at this program? After all the bloody past, are we longer to defy the divine law of justice? Are we still unmindful of the doom which awaits the strong nation which tramples upon the rights of the weak? Shall we not be advised by all history and by our own sense of right that "They shall not rule who refuse to rule in righteousness"? I confess it stirs all the wrath of my being, it disappoints me to think that this Republic is to recognize or take from or advantage in any way by this instrument. I would have striven in every possible way to avoid recognition of that which I conceive to be a conspiracy against justice, against peace, against humanity, and against civilization.

XI

DISARMAMENT CONFERENCE RESOLUTION

The famous resolution looking to the Washington Disarmament Conference was originally introduced by Borah in the 66th Congress, December 14th, 1920. It was re-introduced in the 67th Congress on April 14th, 1921. It was passed June 29th, 1921.

Later, July 10th, 1921, the State Department announced that Great Britain, France and Japan, had "been approached" with a view to considering a conference. The conference was convened the following autumn.

[Extract from Public Document No. 35, 67th Congress.]

Sec. 9. That the President is authorized and requested to invite the Governments of Great Britain and Japan to send representatives to a conference, which shall be charged with the duty of promptly entering into an understanding or agreement by which the naval expenditures and building programs of each of said Governments, to wit, the United States, Great Britain, and Japan, shall be substantially reduced annually during the next five years to such an extent and upon such terms as may be agreed upon, which understanding or agreement is to be reported to the respective Governments for approval.

XII

THE ISSUE OF THE WAR

(Excerpt from Speech in the United States Senate, March 18, 1918.)

Mr. President, I have always believed from the very beginning of the war that the first breakdown in this great conflict will, if any breakdown comes, be in the industrial life and in the agricultural field. The military men who are engaged in taking care of that part of the program will see that we get sufficient men in uniform and that we get sufficient men to the front, but I am afraid they are not disposed to give sufficient attention to those things which are necessary to support the men who are in uniform and who are at the front. It is natural for those who are dealing with that feature of the situation to fasten their time and their attention solely upon the question of man power.

But this is not, as most previous wars have been, a war merely of armies; it is a war of nations; it is a contention and a conflict between whole peoples, and not merely between great armies.

In former times, until the Revolution in France, wars were carried on by armies, which were often employed and dissociated or disunited in a marked degree at least from the nation itself. The war went forward and the battles were fought without very much strain or without very much readjustment of the national life. But this conflict is distinctly a war between nations. It is one people pitted against another. It calls for the resources and the energies and the powers of the people as a whole. No man in this contest can be indifferent to the situation upon the theory that he is not geared up to some activity in connection with the war. Whether he is upon the farm, in the workshop, in the factory, or in the law office, he is in some measure contributing, if he is doing his duty; or, if he is not doing his duty, he is menacing this great conflict in which we are now engaged. So it is incumbent upon us to see to it that we do not break down industrially and agriculturally, as much as it is to see that we do not fail to supply the proper men at the front in France.

Let us reflect for a minute upon this situation as it now confronts us. It will appear more conclusively that this is a war between the nations and the question of victory depends upon which is best organized and best united in spirit and in purpose, industrially and economically. That question will determine who shall win this great conflict.

Germany is now in possession of middle Europe. Bulgaria, Roumania, Austria-Hungary, Turkey, and a large portion of Russia are as completely a part of the German Empire as if national lines were wiped out. She has already realized one of the great objects and purpose of entering this war, which was to establish a middle Europe, to get control of the vast resources in the center of the Continent, and place herself practically in a fortified fortress in the middle of Europe. That is now largely a realization. While we still speak of Austria-Hungary and Turkey and Bulgaria and Roumania, they are as a matter of fact a part of the German Empire, and all orders proceed from Berlin.

The Kaiser is controlling the destinies of those nations as if they had been incorporated as a part of his Empire. Germany is taking possession day by day of the resources of Russia; she either has, or will have before very many months shall have passed, control of all that portion of Russia which she desires to control. With her capacity for organization, her transcendent aptitude for efficiency, in control of middle Europe, and with the natural resources of Russia behind her, this is not, indeed, a war between armies, but a war of nations. It will be determined according to the manner in which we organize ourselves industrially and agriculturally; how we stand economically, and how, as a people, we are united in spirit and in purpose.

You may put upon the western front all the soldiers that you can build ships to carry, but if there is not behind them a united and determined people, aroused and thoroughly understanding the fact that we are all a part of the contest, we shall not be able to succeed in the end. We could do nothing in this contest that would more discourage the German dynasty than to demonstrate once and for all that we are a thoroughly united people, determined to sacrifice whatever it is necessary to sacrifice in order to crush the military power of that people.

And when we reflect further on some of the issues which are involved in the war, we are again led to understand how conclusively this is a contest between the two systems of government, two civilizations. We ought to get away, if we can, from the idea that it is a conflict over national lines in Europe; that it is a question of the redistribution of territory in Europe; that it is a question of securing compensation for injuries which have been done to us; and understand that, whatever the cause was in the beginning, we have now arrived at a point where it is distinctly a conflict between two systems of government, between peoples and nations, and that one or the other will have to go down.

I read yesterday in the New York Times an article appearing within the last thirty days in a leading paper published in Germany, one of the responsible journals of that country, in which it discusses the things that it will be necessary for the United States to concede in the readjustment after the war. Among others, it declares unalterably against the Monroe doctrine, and that neither Germany nor the other European countries with which Germany is associated can longer submit to that doctrine. It also declares against the immigration laws which inhibit certain immigrants coming to this country. Among other things, reading a single extract or two, this article says:

Our leaders builded better than they knew in their decision for unrestricted submarine warfare in that they thus voted that in the name of all Europe our people should confront the Yankeeism hidden in the Monroe doctrine, as if the nations of Europe could in future be excluded from those advantages which Columbus, by his discovery of America, opened up for all time to the civilized world. How little till now has Europe comprehended that the Monroe doctrine in its last analysis signifies nothing less than this.

The war was always, to our way of thinking, a war against America even before it came to the rupture of diplomatic relations and the declaration of a state of war. Nobody doubts that we should have been able much earlier to conclude a favorable peace if the American means of assistance had been at our disposal in the same measure as they have been at the disposal of our enemies or if they had been denied to them as they have been to us. So much more is America, since her openly declared participation in the war, our chief enemy, who alone can galvanize our other enemies to new and bolder resistance. If we can only emerge from this war unvanquished, without giving securities and indemnities, this alone is equivalent to stigmatizing the whole Anglo-Saxon race. The nations who today believe in that race will, when they understand this fact, awake from the trance that let them work and fight so long for the Anglo-Saxon world dominion. In a higher sense even this world war is a war for the faith. There will be no salvation for Anglo-Saxon dominion, either in the British Empire or in America if this process of "crushing" miscarries, to say nothing of the result if it ends in a debacle of the entente.

* * * * * * * *

The Monroe doctrine in the last analysis is nothing but a transfer of the provincial Anglo-Saxon spirit to the New World. In its name, therefore, the principle has been laid down that emigration from the European continent should be tolerated only so far as it corresponds with the endeavor of the old Anglo-American aristocratic families to be self-sufficient and exclusive.

* * * * * * * *

In this the correct sentiment for a continental European community of interests in opposition to the insularity of the Anglo-Saxon race finds expression. From this it is evident that the German policy of supplanting Anglo-Saxonism from its position of world dominion by Germanism can not be better inducted than by emphasizing with all vigor during the war, and especially at the peace negotiations, the interests of pan-Europe against the Monroe doctrine in so far as this doctrine is intended to create ever new difficulties for the sale of European merchandise in American markets, and above all for the emigration of Europeans to any parts of the New World.

In other words, whatever may have been our opinion in the beginning of the war, both sides realize now that this is not only a war between great nations, involving the interests of all their citizens, but it is distinctly a war between systems of Government, and it is so recognized.

The German historian, Prof. Meyer, in a book written since the beginning of the war in which he sums up the issues involved, or rather the issue because it all resolves itself into one, uses this language:

The truth of the whole matter undoubtedly is that the time has arrived when two district forms of State organization must face each other in a life-and-death struggle.

That is undoubtedly the understanding and

belief of those who are responsible for this war.
It is coming to be the understanding and belief
of those who have had the war forced upon
them. We have finally put aside the tragedy
at the Bosnian capital and the wrongs inflicted
upon Belgium as the moving causes of the war.
They were but the prologue to the imperial
theme. We now see and understand clearly
and unmistakably the cause at all times lying
back of these things. Upon the one hand is
Magna Charta, the Bill of Rights, the Declaration of Independence, the Constitution of the
United States, and the principles of human liberty which they embody and preserve. Upon
the other hand is that peculiar form of State
organization which, in the language of the em-
peror, rests alone upon the strength of the
army and whose highest creed finds expression
in the words of one of its greatest advocates
that war is a part of the eternal order instituted
by God. We go back to Runnymede, where
fearless men wrenched from the hands of
power habeas corpus and the trial by jury.
They point us to Breslau and Molwitz,
where Frederick the Great, in violation of his
plighted word, inaugurated the rule of fraud
and force and laid the foundation for that

mighty structure whose central and dominating principle is that of power.

It is that power with which we are at war today. Shall men, shall the people, be governed by some remorseless and soulless entity softly called the "State" or shall the instrumentalities of government yield alone and at all times to the wants and necessities, the hopes and aspirations of the masses? That is now the issue. Nothing should longer conceal it. It is but another and more stupendous phase of the old struggle, a struggle as ancient and as inevitable as the thirst for power and the love of liberty, a struggle in which men have fought and sacrificed all the way from Marathon to Verdun.

It seems strange now, and it will seem more extraordinary to those who come after us, that we did not recognize from the beginning that this was the issue. But, obscured by the débris of European life, confused with the dynastic quarrels and racial bitterness of the Old World, it was difficult to discern, and still more difficult to realize, that the very life of our institutions was at stake, that the scheme of the enemy, amazing and astounding, was not alone to control territory and dominate commerce, but to change the drift of human progress and to readjust the standards of the world's civilization. Perhaps, too, our love of peace, our traditional friendship for all nations lulled suspicion and discouraged inquiry. Be that as it may, there can be no doubt now. Whatever the cause, however perverse the fates which brings us to this crisis, we are called upon not to settle questions of territory or establish new spheres of national activity, but to defend the institutions under which we live. Who doubts should we fail that the whole theory and system of government for which we have labored and struggled, our whole conception of civilization would be discredited utterly. Who but believes that should we lose militarism would be the searching test of all governments and that the world would be an armed camp harried and tortured and decimated by endless wars. No; we can no longer doubt the issue, and, notwithstanding some discouraging facts, we must not doubt the result. We are simply meeting the test which brave men have met before, for this issue has been fought over for three thousand years. Islam's fanacticism was grounded in the same design and made of the same stuff, but it broke upon the valor of Charles Martel's men at Tours. But the conflict was not conclusive. The elder Napoleon was obsessed by the same dream of world dominion, the same passion for military glory that now obsesses those against whom we war. But he, too, saw his universal scepter depart when chance and fate which sometimes war on the side of liberty turned from him on the field of Waterloo. And now the issue is again made up, and again this dream of world dominion, this passion for military glory torments the souls of our would-be masters. And now again somewhere on the battle fields of Europe the same fate awaits the hosts of irresponsible power. In such a contest and with such an issue we can not lose; it would not harmonize with the law of human progress.

It has been the proud belief of some that not only would this war result in greater prestige and greater security for free institutions but that it would effectuate the spread of democracy throughout Europe. We all hope for great things, for we believe in the ultimate triumph of free institutions, but we must not expect these things out of hand. The broken sobs of nations struggling to be independent and free so often heard in that part of the world and then heard no more, the story of Russia just now being written in contention and blood admonishes anew that the republican road to safety and stability is encompassed by all kinds of trials and beset by countless perils. Democracy is the severest test of character which can be put upon a people, and must be earned and acquired in the rigid school of experience. It can not be handed whole and complete to any people, though every member of the community were a Socrates. But what we have determined in this crisis, as I understand it, is that we will keep the road of democracy open. No one shall close it. If any nation shall hereafter rise to the sublime requirement of self-government and choose to go that way it shall have the right to do so. Above all things we have determined, cost what it may in treasure and blood, that this experiment here upon this Western Continent shall justify the faith of its builders, that there shall remain here in all the integrity of its powers neither wrenched nor marred by the passions of war from within nor humbled nor dishonored by millitary power from without the Republic of the fathers. That since the challenge has been thrown down that this is a war unto death between two opposing theories of government we are determined that whatever else happens as a result of this war this form of organization, this theory of state, this last great hope, this fruition of one hundred and thirty years of struggle and toil "shall not perish from the earth."

So, sir, stripped of all incidental and confusing things, the problem which our soldiers will help to solve is whether the theory of government exemplified in the dynasty of the Hohenzollerns or the theory of government exemplified in the faith of Abraham Lincoln shall prevail. It is after all a war of ideas, a clash of systems, a death struggle of ideals. Amid the sacrilege of war it is our belief that the old order passeth. In such a contest there is little room for compromise. We can no more quit than Washington could have quit at Valley Forge. We can no more compromise than Lincoln could have compromised after Chancellorsville. We can and should keep the issue clear of all selfish and imperialistic ambitions, but the issue itself can not be compromised. Cost what it may in treasure and blood the burden, as if by fate, has been laid upon us, and we must meet it manfully and successfully. To compromise is to acknowledge defeat. The policies of Frederick the Great which would make of all human souls mere cogs in a vast military machine, and the policies of Washington which would make government the expression and the instrument of popular power are contending for supremacy on the battle fields of Europe. Just that single, simple, stupendous issue, beside which all other issues in this war are trivial, must have a settlement as clear and conclusive as the settlement at Runnymede or Yorktown. To lose sight of this fact is to miss the supreme purpose of the war, and to permit it to be embarrassed or belittled by questions of territory is to betray the cause of civilization. And to fail to settle it clearly and conclusively is to fail in the most vital and sublime task ever laid upon a people.

We need not prophesy now when victory will come. Neither is it profitable to speculate how it will come. If it is a real and not a sham peace, we shall have no trouble in recognizing it when it does come. Whether it shall come in the bloody and visible triumph of arms or, as we hope, through the overthrow and destruction of militarism by the people of the respective countries, we do not know. But that it will come we confidently believe. Indeed, if the principles of right and the precepts of liberty are not a myth, we know it will come. It has been said by some one that it was not possible for Napoleon to win at Waterloo, not on account of Wellington, not on account of Blucher, but on account of the unchanging laws of liberty and justice. Let us call something of this faith to our own contest. Let us go forward in the belief that it is not possible in the morning of the twentieth century of the Christian civilization for militarism, for brute force, to triumph. It would be in contravention to every law, human and divine, upon which rests the happiness and preservation of the human family. It would be to place brute force first in the divine economy of things. It would be to place might over right, and in the last and final struggle that can not be done. No; we can not lose. We must win. The only question is whether we shall, through efficiency and concerted and united action, win without unnecessary loss of life, unnecessary waste of treasure, or whether we shall, through lack of unity in spirit and purpose, win only after fearful and unnecessary sacrifices.

It has often been said since the war began that a republic can not make war. I trample the doctrine under my feet. I scorn the faithless creed as the creed of cowards and traitors. If a republic can not make war, if it can not stand the ordeal of conflict, why in the name of the living God are our boys on the western front? Are they there to suffer and die for a miserable craft that can only float in the serene breeze of the summer seas and must sink or drive for port at the first coming on of the storm? No; they are there to defend a craft which is equal to every conflict and superior to every foe—the triumph and the pride of all the barks that have battled with the ocean of time. A republic can make war. It can make war successfully and triumphantly and remain a republic every hour of the conflict. The genius who presided over the organiation of this Republic, whose impressive force was knit into every fiber of our international organization, was the greatest soldier, save one, of the modern world, and the most far-visioned leader and statesman of all time. He knew that though devoted to peace the time would come when the Republic would have to make war. Over and over again he solemnly warned his countrymen to be ever ready and always prepared. He intended, therefore, that this Republic should make war and make war effectively, and the Republic which Washington framed and baptized with his love can make war. 'Let these faithless recreants cease to preach their pernicious doctrine.

Sir, this theory, this belief that a self-governing people can not make war without forfeiting their freedom and their form of government is vicious enough to have been kenneled in some foreign clime. A hundred million people knit together by the ties of a common patriotism, united in spirit and purpose, conscious of the fact that their freedom is imperiled, and exerting their energies and asserting their powers through the avenues and machinery of a representative Republic is the most masterful enginery of war yet devised by man. It has in it a power, an element of strength, which no military power of itself can bring into effect. The American soldier, a part of the life of his Nation, imbued with devotion to his country, has something in him that no system or mere military training and discipline as applied to automatoms of an absolute government can ever give. The most priceless heritage which this war will leave to a war-torn and weary world is the demonstrated fact that a free people of a free Government can make war successfully and triumphantly, can defy and defeat militarism and preserve through it all their independence, their freedom, and the integrity of their institutions.

XIII

PUBLIC DEBT

(Excerpt from Speech in the United States Senate, February 17, 1921.)

Mr. President, this debt which now rests like a mortgage in process of everlasting foreclosure upon the brain and the energy of the human family really staggers computation, and in its demoralizing and deadening effect beggars description. We seek to estimate it in figures and speak to each other in terms of billions, but all this signifies but very little. It is when you undertake to measure this debt in foot pounds of human toil that its magnitude becomes bewildering. The privation and the misery, the suffering and the sacrifice, the men and women bending in hopeless drudgery, the children starved in body and stunted in mind, the families discouraged and broken up, the pauperism, the crime, the suicide, which its everpressing weight and subtle tyranny imposes, place its size and its effect beyond our power to portray. The most exacting taskmaster in the world is the public debt. The most remorseless cruelty which a community as a whole can experience is this ceaseless, never-ending struggle to meet its obligation. If it has any advantages to bestow, it bestows them upon the few and well favored—those who are able to hold bonds and collect the interest. But it sits with the average citizen at his meals and accompanies him in his daily avocation to take from him all that he can be persuaded or driven to give and leaves him nothing in return. I have read of theorists who argue that public debts are really a benefit; that at least their evils are greatly exaggerated. I think the public debt a curse. It eats the substance of the people, kills initiative, undermines and corrupts society, breeds discontent and disorder, and often destroys government itself. The immediate and most commanding task of all those who would see a composed world and prosperous and orderly communities and States is to devise ways and means to reduce it if possible, and in the name of humanity to see that it goes no higher.

XIV

MILITARISM

(Excerpt from Speech in the United States Senate, February 17, 1921.)

When the war ended, Germany was disabled; her army was reduced to a police force; her navy dismantled, broken up, sunk into the depths of the sea. Austria-Hungary was divided, parceled out, driven into bankruptcy and starvation. No nation, no power among the enemy anywhere was left to threaten or make afraid. The allied and associated powers were left masters of the world, dictators of the world's policies. They were the autocrats of statecraft. While they surveyed a world torn, tortured, and burdened, they nevertheless surveyed it without challenge. The most stupendous fact at the close of the war was the world debt. The most pressing and complex problem was how to stay its growth and, if possible, lessen its weight. But no move was made, nor has there been any move made in that direction in any of the allied or associated countries. The futile and absurd proposition that the cost of the war and the world's debt could be extracted from Germany was flaunted before the people, while the expenditures for militarism and armaments were increased beyond anything ever before contemplated. With incontinent haste and reckless plunging we began to compete with each other in building for future wars. With our huge debt already upon us, with our current expenses greater than we dare lay taxes to cover, we surge ahead—plunge ahead toward universal bankruptcy. When are we going to lighten these burdens? How are we going to do it? Where is the program? Have we lost our cunning in everything in God's tortured world save that of appropriating public money? There must be a change of program some time, and in my judgment at no distant time.

The news dispatches advise us that before convening Parliament a few days since it was thought the part of safety to barricade, as it were, the streets and avenues leading to the House of Commons. Of course, it was immediately said that it was to guard against Sinn Feiners. But it now transpires that there was another factor in the situation, to wit, the discontented, hungry, unemployed workmen of England. In Japan the spirit of unrest and revolt is stirring everywhere among the masses as never before. In our own country business is worried and discouraged by crushing taxes, while 3,000,000 workmen are seeking employment. Taxes and appropriations, appropriations and taxes, will not cure such conditions. It is not a long step from the barricade around the legislative halls and unemployment to the point where popular power breaks in upon the rights of property and decrees are issued from the open forum. Unjust and oppressive taxation—this will destroy the morale of the most self-poised and patient people in the world and shake the foundation of the most noble and freest institution ever devised by sage or patriot. I ask again, and I ask in deep sincerity, if the suggestions and remedies I have proposed are inadequate, what is the program? What do we propose to do? To drift is a confession of sheer incompetency. The path of mere expediency is the path to disaster. If the program proposed is unavailing, then what is the program?

XV

RECALL OF JUDGES

(Excerpt from Speech in the United States Senate, August 7, 1911.)

Mr. President, I maintain that in writing a law, in placing upon the statute books a guide or rule of action for men, we ought to listen closely to the instructions of a well-formed and well-sustained public opinion. I am aware that the complex and involved conditions of modern questions require much study and long training upon the part of the successful legislator. But this is only a part of the equipment and only a part of that which should go into the law. Upon no question with which we deal here can we afford to ignore that wholesome, practical wisdom born of the reflection and experience of 90,000,000 people. It is a remarkably safe guide. It has served this country well when wise statesmen seemed powerless to determine upon a policy. It has in it something of that strength, that saving common sense, that intuitive sense of equity and justice not always found outside of the great forum where men gather wisdom in the actual struggle for existence. The law should embody in its enactment not only the technical skill and more profound insight of the trained legislator but it should embody as nearly as may be the practical information of the railroad owner and the laborer, of the banker and the farmer, the merchant and the lawyer, and the countless thousands upon whose integrity and industry rests the whole vast fabric of modern business and out of whose experience must come also our humane and beneficent policies.

But after the law is written the man who construes it, and by its terms measures out to each citizen his duty or his obligation, should consider nothing but the terms of the law as written. He has nothing to do with its leniency or its harshness, its wisdom or its unwisdom. He is not to consider the effect of its enforcement unless it be when there is doubt as to its terms. He can not consider his own interest, he can not seek the advice of friends, and he can serve the people in no other way than by faithfully construing the law which the people, through the law-making department, have written. Though the public welfare, the public interest, and public sentiment seem to be on one side and only the legal rights of an humble, obscure citizen upon the other, his duty is still the same.

He is an unworthy judge if he considers otherwise. He must reply to all influences, be they private or public, as the chief justice replied to the English king who sent to know if he would consult with him before rendering his decision: "When the cause is submitted I will decide as becomes the chief justice of England." If the law be a bad law, detrimental to the public welfare, the people may modify or repeal it. But the judge who legislates not only violates his oath, but undermines the basic principles of our institutions and opens the door to injustice and fraud.

The most paltry being who slimes his way through the machinery of government is the judge who seeks to locate the popular side of a justiciable controversy. The man of small fortune or limited means will always suffer in a contest with influence or wealth in such a court. Instead of a trial, if he has a just cause, he will get demurrers and postponements, costs, and that delay which in the end constitutes a denial of justice. How many lawyers representing a poor or obscure client have not heard the client breathe a prayer of relief if it could be said to him, "This judge before whom you are going will decide absolutely as he sees the law; the influence of your antagonist will not affect him." Unless a judge is corrupt or in some such way at fault, which things may always be dealt with under the law, I want him to know when he takes his oath that he is to serve the stated time for which he has been elected or chosen. I want him to feel and know that for that length of time he can walk unafraid in constant company with his own conscience and follow, without fear or favor, the light of his own intellect. The distribution of justice is the most solemn and most difficult task which government imposes upon men. Human nature is weak for the task at best. Remembering this, we should not impose upon those who are called to this high service our selfishness, our objections, our prejudices, our partisanship, unrestrained by their oath or their obligations, unsteadied by their sense of responsibility. We should rather brace and prop them for the work in a way best calculated to inspire courage, confidence, and independence. It is my deliberate and uncompromising opinion that without a free, untrammeled, independent judiciary popular government, the government of the people, by the people, and for the people, would be a delusion—a taunting, tormenting delusion. This is the unbroken record from the dicasteries of Athens to the mimic tribunals of justice which are found to-day in some of the Republics to the south.

I am afraid that the principle of the recall as applied to judges will tend to establish the rule of the majority in matters of judicial controversy. It will tend to make decisions bear the color and drift of majority rule or party domination rather than that of a faithful rendition of the law and the facts. What is the basic principle of democratic or republican government? We sometimes urge that the first principle is that the majority shall rule. That is true in making laws and determining policies, but it has no place in and will destroy republican government if applied to the courts or to controversies to be determined under the law. There all men are equal. Back of the rule of the majority is the great principle of equality, the basic, bedrock principle of free government. The difference between the old democracies or republics, which perished, and ours, is that the ancient republics could devise no way by which to shield the rights of the minority. Though the majority must rule, yet a government which has no method for protecting the rights of the minority—for it has rights —is a despotic government, I do not care whether you call it a monarchy, an aristocracy, or a republic. A government which will not protect me in my rights, though I stand alone and against all my neighbors, is a despotic government. If our courts are taught to listen, trained by this subtle process of the years to hearken to the voice of the majority, to whom will the minority appeal for relief? If the voice of the majority controls, if this principle finally comes to be recognized in the timidity of judges, to what power in our Government will the isolated, the unfortunate, the humble, and the poor go for relief? Where will those without prestige, without wealth or social rank go for protection?

It is easy, in our zeal to put forward under the guise of popular government things which will challenge the saneness or practicability of the entire movement and thus bring discredit and defeat to great and important measures. It is indispensable to the success of all efforts to secure results for the people that we should distinguish at all times in proposed changes between that which experience has proven to be evil and that which experience has proven to be good. We must not mistake the mere spirit of reckless change for the throes of progress. The intellectual capital of a single decade is too small upon which to proceed to the business of

changing the fundamental basis of government
—we must add to it the accumulated experience of all the past. Many a splendid movement for better government has become sur-
feited with an excess of ecstasy and thus sur-
feiting "sicken and so die." It requires just as
much judgment, coolness, and persistency, just
as much common sense, just as shrewd and
keen a regard for the common experience and
the peculiar qualities of human nature to
achieve good legislation for the people as it
does to enact the bad. When we take an unwise or an impractical position we have contributed something to the victory of the opposition.

There is a vast amount of practical common
sense in the ordinary American citizen. He is
never long in error. He loves liberty, but he
also in the end demands security and stability.
He would not long accept a proposition which
would imperil the stability and independence of
the judicial system for which his ancestors
fought for three centuries. One of the main
questions settled by the English revolution of
1688 was that the people should have the right
to appeal for protection to an independent tribunal of justice. Prior to that time the judges
were subject to removal by the King. Under

this power he took some of the keenest intellects and brightest minds of the English bar and made of them the corrupt and willing instruments of oppression and injustice. Rather than to go before such a tribunal Essex took his own life in the tower. Under this system Pemberton was appointed, that he might preside at the trial of Russel, and was then recalled because his instructions, though strikingly unfair and partial, were not sufficiently brutal to satisfy the insatiable monster who had given him his soiled and polluted ermine. Under such a system the martyr of English liberty, Sydney, was beheaded; freedom of speech was destroyed, habeas corpus denied, and individual rights trampled under foot. So when the English yeomanry drove their monarch from the throne they wrote into the terms of the "act of settlement" that "judges' commissions be made during good behavior and their salary ascertained and established." This took it out of the power of the King to remove the judges and out of his power to impoverish them by withholding their salary. This was the first step toward an independent judiciary, and it was not long until the great English orator could truly say, in speaking of this to the English people:

Though it was but a cottage with a thatched roof which the four winds could enter, the King could not.

Thereafter, instead of Jeffreys denouncing and cursing from the bench the aged Baxter, instead of Dudley taunting and tormenting the New England colonists, instead of Scroggs and Saunders, subtle and dextrous instruments of tyranny, we have Somers and Holt, and York and Hardwick, and Eldon and Mansfield laying deep and firm the great principles of English law and English justice, principles which still shield and guard the personal rights of every member of the English-speaking race, principles which our fathers were careful to bring here, principles which every American citizen would unhesitatingly shoulder his musket to defend and preserve.

No less fruitful of great names and commanding figures has been the system in our own country. Jay and Marshall, Taney and Kent and Story and that line of judges, reaching down to the distinguished and cultured Chief Justice who now presides over the Supreme Court. The intellect, the character, the best there was in these men of heart and mind, years of consecration and toil, are embedded in our jurisprudence, and constitute today the greatest of all guaranties for the perpetuity of our institutions and the continued happiness and prosperity of the common people.

Sir, it seems to me that the experience of the past has closed the discussion as to the necessity of an independent judiciary. A feeble, a timid, an obedient judiciary, whether to popular demand or king, has always in the end proven to be an incompetent, a cruel, or a corrupt judiciary. Such a judiciary leaves human rights uncertain and worthless, unsettles titles, destroys values, leaves the workman and the employer alike without protection or guidance, and has more than once demoralized or destroyed governments. Trade, commerce, or labor have never, and will never, flourish or prosper under an unstable and unreliable system of courts. Whether you look upon the wreck of ancient republics and democracies where the courts yielded their decisions to the triumphant faction or party or to modern monarchies where the miserable instruments of kingly power served well their master, whenever and wherever in all history you find a dependent judiciary you find that it is the man of limited means, the poor man, who suffers first and suffers most—the man who has not the wealth to purchase immunity or the prestige to command decrees.

If there is any man in the world who is interested in having a brave, able, fearless, independent judiciary, judges who will, as against influence or power, political or financial, interpret the law as it is written, it is the man of limited or no means. His small holding, the honor of his name, his liberty, even his life, may be in jeopardy. If so, does he want a judge who will listen to wealthy friends or political advisers? Does he want to approach a tribunal above which rests the threat of political humiliation or punishment? Does he want to meet in court some political dictator? I repeat, the man of influence, of means, may contend against such odds, but the humble citizen without prestige or wealth can not do so. We owe it to ourselves and to posterity, to the institutions under which we live, and above all to the common people of this country, to see to it that our judiciary is placed, as nearly as human ingenuity can do so, beyond the reach of influence or any of the things which may cloud the mind with passion or fear or dull the conscience to the highest demands of even-handed justice.

In order that what we do for the people may be permanent and beneficial, in order that our honest purposes may not come back cursed with frailty and impotency, let us not ignore the plainest dictates of reason and the soundest principles evoked out of all these years of experience. While we pursue with unwonted zeal the abstract rights of man we are at the same time bound to remember man's nature. We want liberty and popular government, to be sure; but unless these are accompanied with wisdom and justice, unless there goes along with all reforms the homely, practical, common sense which takes notice of man's vices as well as his virtues our efforts will end at last in the misery of failure. When the people have written the law, then let us have an independent judge, free from any political fear, to interpret the law as written until the people rewrite it. The people's courts can no more survive the demoralizing effect of the vices of majorities in the administration of justice than the king's courts could stand against the influence of their masters.

Sir, we can never, never afford to forget that a republic, too, must have its element of stability—its fundamental law and its independent judiciary to construe and apply it. A democracy can not be as changeful as the moods of a day and long endure. A republic must have in it the element of respect and reverence, of devotion to its institutions and loyalty to its traditions. It, too, must have its altars, its memory of sacrifices—something for which men are willing to die. If the time ever comes when the fundamental principles of our Government as embodied in our Constitution no longer hold the respect and fealty of a majority of our people popular government will, as a practical fact, not long survive that hour. The poorer classes, the overworked and humble, those without wealth, influence, and standing will cry for rest and find it in any form of government which can give it to them. I look upon an independent judiciary as the very keystone to the arch of popular government. Without it the wit of man never has and never can devise a popular scheme of government that will long protect the rights of the ordinary citizen.

I have often thought if there is a sacred spot on the face of God's footstool made so by the institutions of man it is in front of the tribunal where presides the Chief Justice of the United States. There you may take the poorest, the most unfortunate individual in the land and he is heard, heard, sir, as if he stood clothed with all the influence which wealth and friends could bestow. Though he stands there with every, man's hand against him and every right denied, that tribunal throws about him the guaranties and protection of the Constitution, the fundamental law which the people have made for the protection of all, and he stands upon an equality with every other man in the land. Even though he be too impecunious to file a brief, with no less care will those painstaking and overworked and devoted men examine into and determine his cause. And if in the end judgment shall be rendered in his favor, if need be the power of this Union will enforce its terms. Do we appreciate the worth of this tribunal and the great underlying principles which have made it what it is? Do we understand how this Government of ours without this steadying, stable, immovable tribunal of justice would go to pieces in a decade? A decade, Mr. President! Rather should we say to all practical effects it would depart in a night. Not a court beyond the possibility of error, not a court whose opinions are to be deemed above the reach of fair and honest criticism, but a court which, whether viewed as to the reach and scope and power of its jurisdiction or as to its influence and standing, its ability and learning, its dedication and consecration to the service of mankind, is the greatest tribunal for order and justice yet created among men.

I sympathize fully and I want to cooperate at all times with those who would make the political side of our Government more responsive and more obedient to the demands of the people. I know that changed conditions demand a change in the details of our Government upon its political side. But the rules by which men who distribute justice are to be governed and the influences which embarrass them in this high work are the same now and will always be the same as they have ever been. Let us not impeach the saneness and the worth of our great cause by challenging the great and indispensable principle of an independent judiciary. Let us not mislead the people into the belief that their interests or their welfare lie in the direction of justice tempered with popular opinion. Let us not draw these tribunals, before which must come the rich and the poor, the great and the small, the powerful and the weak, closer, even still closer, than now, to the passions and turmoils of politics. Let us cling to this principle of an independent judiciary as of old they would cling to the horns of the altar.

XVI

THE ALTERNATIVE

(Excerpt from Speech in the United States Senate, August 19, 1914.)

It is a common, and, I think, a deplorably common thing in these days to be always assailing the courts. I do not sympathize with this wholesale assault.

I do not claim that the courts do not err; they sometimes err signally and pronouncedly. I do not claim that they always administer justice with an even and exact hand, for judges are human and the passions and prejudices, the limited vision and the clouded mind which sometimes attach to their kind are also theirs. I do not claim that they are always free from political bias or at all times wholly exempt from that strange attachment which in a republic sometimes places party above the common welfare, for Presidents and governors and electorates in selecting judges do not always seek men most likely to resist such influences. But I do claim that of all the methods and contrivances and schemes which have been devised by the wit of man for the adjustment of controverted judicial questions and the administration of justice the courts and the machinery of the courts, built up from decade to decade and from century to century, built of the experience and the wisdom of a proud and freedom-loving race, the courts as they are built into our system, though not perfect, are the most perfect. They will not always be abreast of the most advanced opinions in the march of progress, but that they will in due time mortise and build into our jurisprudence all that is permanent and wise and just, all that a settled and digested public opinion finally indorses, no one familiar with the history of our jurisprudence can for a moment doubt. Not only that, but more than once the courts, both in England and America, have stood as the sole protector in the hour of turmoil and strife for the rights of the weak and the poor, the oppressed and the hunted, when the executive and the legislature have yielded to the whip of the strong and the powerful. I need recall only one instance in the hurry of this debate, though I might recall a hundred, beginning with the days of Coke's courage, and that is the instance wherein our own great Supreme Court preserved against the encroachments of war and the hunger of hatred the right of trial by jury, a most sacred right of the American citizen and without which the whole scheme of a republic would be but a delusion and a torment.

After the courts then what? When the courts can no longer stay the steps which may lead to violence and bloodshed, then what? When the arm of equity can no longer be extended to hold things in abeyance until rights can be adjudicated and reason and counsel can have a hearing, then what? Be not deceived. The alternative is the soldier and the bayonet. One can not be oblivious to the alacrity with which wealth in these days is prone to appeal to the soldier. When a delegation of workingmen informed me a few months ago that their fellow workmen had been arrested without warrant, tried without a jury, sentenced by no court—that at a time when the courts were open and in the midst of an intelligent, prosperous, modern American community men had been herded before a military tribunal, given the semblance of a trial, and sent to prison, it seemed incredible. For six hundred years no such repulsive scene had marred the story of the orderly development and growth of Anglo-Saxon jurisprudence. Our English ancestors had executed the petty tyrants who had last attempted it. I did not suppose that here, where jury trials and common-law courts were a guaranty —a part of our system of law and justice—that anyone would be so blind, so cruel, so witless as to covet the infamy of rehabilitating that discarded and detested dogma—the power of suspension. Nevertheless it was true. Since that time, in three other States, the working-man has settled his troubles out of court where counsel may be heard and witnesses testify, settled them at the point of the bayonet. What a glutton arbitrary power is for the rights and the interests of the weak. It generally comes forward at the bidding of the rich and the pow-erful and preys upon the interests and rights of the poor and the helpless.

These men who came to me were asking for what? They were asking for a hearing in the courts, before this tribunal, whose judgments they informed me they were willing to take. They were praying for the common-law court and its machinery just as it had been worked out and fought for in the humble days of our English ancestors to the humble days of their descendants on Paint and Cabin Creek in one of the great Commonwealths of this Union. And what was the answer to the charge when we arrived upon the ground? When we asked why have these men charged with offenses under the statute and guaranteed a trial in a common-law court been denied the right of the humblest citizen when charged with crime, what was the answer? The answer was not that riot and war had closed the courts, but that excitement and feeling in the community would render them ineffective in all probability. When we inquired further, the fear was that these laboring men would likely be acquitted. What, before the courts, acquitted under the processes and according to the manner that guilty men have been punished and innocent men acquitted for ten centuries? Then they must be innocent. But the logic seemed to be that, guilty or innocent, they must be punished. Force must be established and certainty as to results must be had. So, the strong fled from the courts of justice, suspended—what an infamous lie—yes, suspended by force the constitution of the State and the Nation, selected a military tribunal, called the judges from the guards who were in charge of the prisoners, tried them in groups, and sent them in droves to the penitentiary. Do not the workingmen understand that in the end their fight will be to maintain these courts in all their purity, independence, and strength? Do they not understand that if we can not have somewhere an independent tribunal free from the passions and conflicts of contestants to distribute justice civilization must do again what it has done in the past—crumble and fall? Does not the average citizen of this country, whoever and wherever he is, understand that in the end he must find justice here in these tribunals or not find it at all? Does he not understand that after they are gone and law and order have departed he will shortly come to be the victim of violence and cruelty and injustice, the plaything of arbitrary power?

There comes a time, when every man and when the people in every walk of life seek shelter under the calm, determined, beneficent power of a great government, rely upon its impartial strength, and accept with gratitude its means and methods of measuring and distributing justice. Men should seek to build a government which has no classes, grants no special privileges, recognizes no creed, and fosters no religion. It is a blind and shortsighted policy to suppose that you can curtail the functions of government in order to bestow favors, for when you have done so you have already weakened government for the prevention of wrongs. The fruits of industry, the wages of the toiler, the income of capital are all affected, fostered, encouraged, and sustained to the extent that order and law obtain throughout the land. While a strong and fearless government may sometimes seem quick to prevent those steps and block those paths which seem to lead to violence and bloodshed, yet ultimately the benefits to flow from such procedure must redound to the peace and happiness, the contentment and prosperity of the whole people. It was Liebknecht, the great socialist, who truly said, "Violence has been for thousands of years a reactionary factor." Show me a country without courts fully equipped in every way to deal with all the intricacies of each particular case as the facts appear, show me a country with its business and industry under the clamp of bureaucracy, its courts weakened, cowardly, and powerless, and I will show you a country where the laborer is no better than a slave— the miserable, ignorant, unclad dupe and plaything of arbitrary power.

XVII

RESOLUTION IN REGARD TO RUSSIA

(Mr. Borah submitted the following resolution in the Senate of the United States, April 20, 1922, which was ordered to lie on the table.)

Resolved, That the Senate of the United States favors the recognition of the present Soviet Government of Russia.

XVIII

RECOGNITION OF RUSSIA

(Speech in the United States Senate, February 21, 1923.)

I presume our frends who are anxious to see the pending bill become a law are interested in having some cargoes for the ships after they have been induced to put to sea. I am much more interested in finding something to put on the ships than I am in the subsidy. There are idle ships in every port in the world for want of cargo to carry. The most vital problem which we can have for consideration is the method or the policy by means of which possibly we may open the markets and find goods to carry, or create a demand which will induce the carriage.

I shall discuss at this time a subject which the friends of the measure may not be willing to admit bears directly upon the question, but certainly it bears on it, as least indirectly. It is certainly of much concern to those who are interested in reopening the markets of Europe to the products which are now a surplus upon our hands.

Upon the 17th day of March, 1917, the last of the Romanoffs abdicated. Immediately thereafter was formed what was known as the provisional government of Russia. That continued until about November 7, 1917, when the Kerensky government or the provisional government was supplanted by what has since been known as the Soviet Government of Russia. That Government has now been in existence going on six years—will have been in existence six years in the coming November.

The policy of the Allies and associated powers toward Russia is incomprehensible except upon the theory that it was thought wise to force back upon the Russian people the rule of the old régime or else dismember and break up Russia into small States. If this or either of these was the policy of the Allies, the course which has been pursued for the last three or four years is indeed understandable. Otherwise it is to me incomprehensible.

Upon the 8th day of January, 1918, the President of the United States made this announcement:

The evacuation of all Russian territories (as one of the conditions in the settlement of the war) and a settlement of all Russian questions such as to insure the best and most untrammeled cooperation of other nations of the world in order to afford Russia a clear and precise opportunity for the independent settlement of her autonomous political development and of her national policy, promising here a cordial welcome in the League of Nations under institutions of her own choice, and, besides a cordial welcome, help and assistance in all that she may need and require. The treatment meted out to Russia by the sister nations in the months to come must be a decisive proof of their good will, of their understanding of her needs as apart from their own interests and of their intelligent and disinterested sympathy.

So far as that outlined a policy upon the part of this Government toward Russia, it seemed to me at the time to state a sound proposition, and it seems to me to be equally sound at the present time—to permit Russia to work out a system of government of her own choosing, to enable her to adopt such policies and pursue such course, so far as her internal affairs are concerned, as the people of Russia, however expressed, might choose. Why that policy has been changed or why it has undergone such a radical departure from the original announcement I am unable to state. I am very thoroughly satisfied, however, that in so far as we have departed it has been error upon our part. I am equally satisfied that should we have pursued a different course than the course which was there outlined the conditions in Russia and the conditions with reference to Russia and the other nations of Europe and the world would have been very much more satisfactory than they are at the present time.

But a little different course prevailed. Immediately after the signing of the armistice there began a rigid, persistent blockade of Russia. It might have been designed to bring about a change of government in Russia. It might have been intended for this or that purpose. I hesitate to say that it was intended as a matter of punishment. But whatever the design and whatever the purpose, it accomplished nothing within the realm of reason or justice in international affairs. Instead of weakening, it strengthened those who were in control of affairs in Russia. Instead of undermining, it strengthened the Bolshevists. Instead of punishing those whom it might be supposed it was thought proper to punish, it punished those who were perfectly helpless to protect themselves. It visited untold misery and suffering upon the masses of the Russian people. Even hospital ships were denied admission to the ports of Russia, a thing indefensible from the standpoint of policy or humanitarianism. It was a cruel, ruthless, futile policy, without conscience or common sense behind it.

After the policy with reference to the blockade came the organization of invasion of Russia by outside powers. The forces of Kolchak and of Wrangel and of Denikin were munitioned and financed by outside powers, by those who had been associated with Russia or with whom Russia had been associated only a short time before. These men represented, in the estimation of the Russian people, the old régime. The peasantry, the masses of Russia, looked upon Kolchak and Wrangel as representatives of the old Czar rule, and that their admission to power or the placing of them in power would be but another way of calling back the old rule. So they failed in their purpose; but while they failed to obtain control of affairs in Russia the invasion succeeded in adding demoralization to the Russian situation and greater and deeper misery to the Russian people. Wide spaces of territory were laid waste. War was again pushed upon a people who had been in war for years, and it would be difficult to calculate the great evil brought to the Russian people by reason of those invasions or attacks munitioned and supplied by outside powers.

The result of the policies thus pursued is at the present time bearing fruit in a way that no one could wish to have it. If the policies which have been pursued should finally ripen into what is now indicated, an understanding or combination between Germany and Russia, and possibly Islam, it would present a condition of affairs quite as serious, so far as the peace of the world is concerned, as that which was presented in August, 1914. If the disciplining and organizing power of Germany should unite with the man power of Russia, and the two should be aided by the fanaticism of Islam, it would present as serious a situation as ever confronted Europe in its entire history. And yet that is the legitimate fruit of the policies which have obtained with reference to both Russia and Germany, one of them dealt with as an outlaw by all the nations who were dominant upon the side of the Allies, and the other dealt with in a way which naturally, as Lloyd-George said at Genoa, has bound them together in bonds of despair, and there they are at the present time.

I read a paragraph from an editorial in the Brooklyn Eagle of a few days since:

[From the Brooklyn Daily Eagle.]

FROM ESSEN TO RUSSIA.

While the French were completing their plans for the seizure of Essen the Krupp firm closed a contract with the Soviet Government for the peaceful invasion of Russia. In the most important concession yet issued by the Lenin-Trotski administration the Krupps obtained the right to exploit some 250,000 acres of rich agricultural land in southwestern Russia which was an appanage of the Russian Crown.

The Krupps are sending to Russia a staff of technicians provided with the most modern agricultural machinery. The machines are of the tractor type. They are being turned out in factories which supplied German tanks during the war. The Krupps propose to create a model farm, operated on the most scientific principles. After some wrangling the Soviet Government has conceded the right to export from Russia whatever this land can be made to produce.

And while the French are destroying Germany's capacity to pay with their bootless invasion of the Ruhr the Russo-Asiatic Bank is supplying British capital with the consent of the British Government in order that the Krupps may develop this new market for their merchandise.

Russia's huge land areas have never been properly exploited. The Germans have the agricultural experts and the plants to produce machines which could quintuple Russian production in a decade. The British are wise enough to realize that here is an ideal field for German development. It creates the markets for their manufactured products which they must have; it supplies them with a part of the food they must purchase abroad; it provides no cutthroat competition in existing world markets.

The editorial is based upon news dispatches which had preceded it several days, which disclosed the fact that those two great people were coming together, combining the respective powers, the natural resources and the man power of the one, the technical knowledge and the disciplining of the other, a thing which it was known to have been taking place for the last two years, although strenuously and repeatedly denied in this country. Does anyone look upon such a condition of affairs without the deepest apprehension? * * *

This is not, as I intimated a moment ago, a new development by any means. Those who have undertaken to watch the effect of the policy of the Allies toward Russia have known for the last two and one-half years that those two great powers were coming together—driven together. It is not a natural combination; it is not a natural condition of affairs. Some antipathies and some antagonisms of more than ordinary moment had to be overcome. The true policy, the wise policy would have preserved the friendship which had long existed between the Russian people and the people of the United States and would have preserved our friendly relations with that power which is now being driven by reason of this condition of affairs into alliance with other nations.

I call attention to a paragraph or two from an article which appeared in L'Echo de Paris, a clerical daily, published in France on March 8, 1922, which reads as follows:

Germany began as early as 1919, to make overtures for business relations with the Soviet Government.

And we ought to bear in mind as we go along that one of the reasons assigned for our failure to do business with Russia is because it was unsafe as a business proposition—

She believed that, although the chaos in Russia might prevent her realizing at once her ultimate political projects in that country, she might open a profitable market there for her manufactures, that would be paid for in gold, precious stones, and the raw materials that Russia still had in stock. It was with this object in view that Germany sent an investigating committee to that country.

* * * * * * * *

after February, 1921, there was rapid progress. From this month, in fact, dates the resumption of commercial intercourse between German and Soviet Russia. On the 18th of February a protocol was signed at Moscow by representatives of the German foreign office and of the Soviet foreign office to regulate provisionally relations between the two countries. Commercial delegations were to be attached to the delegations already established at Moscow and Berlin in order to insure free intercourse between the two nations. Among other things, this agreement regulated passports and visés required of citizens of either country when traveling in the other. It guaranteed the inviolability of the property of Germans who might settle in Russia, with the permission of the soviet authorities, in order to engage in business there.

Again, says the article:

On the 11th of January the Rosta, or official Russian telegraph bureau, announced that after the 6th of that month the German National Bank and the Dresden Bank had agreed to recognize the drafts of the Soviet National Bank. At the same time the Soviet National Bank directed its representatives in Berlin to deposit several million marks with the German National Bank. The same day the Soviet National Bank drew its first check against the German National Bank for 15,000,000 marks. Thus, after an interruption of more than seven years, banking relations were restored between Russia and Germany.

The first fruit gathered from this policy, therefore, is the coming together of these two great powers. If they were associating themselves as friendly nations would ordinarily do, having no antagonism and no reason for antagonism with other nations, it would be a very desirable thing to see; but when we realize that they are brought together, in a large measure, by reason of the policy obtaining against both of those powers, thereby creating a certain state of mind upon the part of these vast peoples, it presents an entirely different aspect and one not at all desirable. I say it is the fruit of this narrow-visioned, intolerant policy—a policy which has borne no fruit save that of hunger, misery, estrangement, and may now be conducive to war. I challenge anyone to point to one single advantage, to one benefit, to one fruitful gathering from this policy. It has been a vindictive policy, and such policies are always barren of good results. My interest in this question from the beginning has been not that of recognition of the Soviet Government because of any sympathy with the principles upon which that government may be founded, nor, indeed, because I believed it would ever in its present form or in the form which first obtained ultimately succeed; but leaving that for them to work out for themselves, the wiser policy, it seemed to me, after the war had closed, was to hold the friendliest possible relations, considering our interests, with this great nation and also with Germany.

Think for a moment of the country which has been outlawed; its population; what it means among the nations of the world and its place among the family of nations as a power when measured by its population and its natural resources. There are in Russia 140,000,000 people—a very industrious, law-abiding, home-loving people, so far as 95 per cent of them are concerned—a people holding the utmost friendliness toward the people of the United States and toward this Government. Russia has an area of 8,166,130 square miles, and, including Khiva and Bokhara, her area is 8,273,130 square miles.

Continental United States has only 3,026,-789 square miles, and, including all our territory, continental and insular, 3,743,510—a little less than half the area of a people who are now outlaws among the nations of the world. It can not be a healthy condition of affairs; and if there is a possible way of avoiding such a condition it is our highest duty, in the interest of peace and in the interest of the restoration of sane economic conditions throughout Europe and the world, to avoid it. It can not be other than a menace to the peace of the entire world that a vast people, with vast natural resources and undoubtedly a great future, are outlawed among the nations. Prior to the war Russia comprised one-sixth of the entire land surface of the globe, and her mineral and timber wealth constituted the greatest undeveloped natural resources in the world.

I can understand why it is to the interest of certain powers in Europe to retard the development of Russia. It is not an interest with which I could have any possible sympathy; but, nevertheless, it is such an interest as has predominated to a marked degree in the foreign policies of European nations. I can understand why powers would organize to finance Denikine and Wrangel to break up and destroy the Russian Government or else restore the old régime, but that ought not to be a policy with which the United States could have any possible sympathy. It is not in the interest of humanity and it is certainly not in the interest of the material welfare of the people either of Russia or of the United States.

There seems to be a popular belief—I do not assume, of course, that it obtains in the State Department—that in recognizing a government we, in a measure, approve of the form of government which the people of that government may have at the time of the recognition. I have received an abundance of letters from people of more or less intelligence which say the recognition of Russia would set the stamp of approval by the United States upon that particular form of government which the Russian people are said at this time to have. Such recognition is not an approval or a disapproval of the form of government; it is a recognition of the fact that they have a government.

It is not an approval of their form of government, any more than our recognition of Turkey today is an approval of the Turkish form of government or of her acts under it. We, finding a people with a government which they have established, recognize as a fact that a government has been established and invite them to become members of the family of nations by the act of recognition.

Woolsey, in his International Law, says:

The question of a State's right to exist is an internal one, to be decided by those within its borders who belong to its organization. To bring the question before external powers not only destroys sovereignty but must either produce perpetual war or bring on the despotism of some one strong nation or strong confederacy of nations, requiring all others to conform their constitutions to the will of these tyrants.

If a nation, or set of nations, should act on the plan of withholding their sanction from new nations with certain constitutions, such a plan would justify others who thought differently in refusing to regard the former any longer as legitimate States.

If we should decline to recognize Russia because of her form of government, and should carry that principle into practice it would necessarily require us to refuse recognition to or withdraw recognition from several nations which I might name.

So far, therefore, as the government from an internal standpoint is concerned, outside of the relationship which it may have with the governments of the earth in its foreign affairs, it is not of the slightest concern to the people of the United States or to the Government of the United States what kind of a government it is. If we shall find in this discussion that, notwithstanding its form of government, it is prepared to discharge its obligations to the other nations of the world, to meet the relationship, and in good faith to discharge the obligations which rest upon it, it is, I say, not of the slightest concern to us what their particular form of government may be.

We are inclined to forget. Our memories are short. It has not been very long in the life of nations, as we measure the life of nations, since the representatives of this Republic were pathetically hunting their way about the courts of Europe, and being rejected for the same reason that is assigned here—that the young Republic was not prepared to meet its obligations or discharge its duties toward the other nations of the world. Think of Franklin and Jay and Adams going about the courts of Europe, almost kicked from pillar to post, and told that "You have no government. Your obligations we can not expect to be carried out. Your treaties will not be fulfilled." Such were the circumstances and such was the faith of great powers who looked upon the formation of a great, free government.

John Fiske, in that perfectly fascinating volume in which he recounts what he calls the critical period of American history, has a paragraph which it may not be out of place to read:

Jefferson, at Paris, was told again and again that it was useless for the French Government to enter into any agreement with the United States, as there was no certainty that it would be fulfilled on our part—

That is, on the part of the United States—

and the same things were said all over Europe. * * * We were bullied by England, insulted by France and Spain, and looked askance at in Holland. The humiliating position in which our ministers were placed by the beggarly poverty of Congress was something almost beyond credance. It was by no means unusual for the superintendent of finance, when hard pushed for money, to draw upon our foreign ministers and then sell the drafts for cash. This was only not unusual; it was an established custom. It was done again and again when there was not the smallest ground for supposing that the minister upon whom the draft was made would have any funds wherewith to meet it. He must go and beg for money. That was part of his duty as envoy, to solicit loans without security for a government that could not raise enough money by taxation to defray its current expenses.

I hope we have heard enough about the fact that after six years this government in Russia is unable to meet its obligations; that it has no money; that it may any day fail or fall by the wayside. That is not a matter, under present conditions and circumstances, which ought to weigh in the least.

The preponderating, controlling, dominating fact is that there is a government which has had an existence for nearly six years, performing all the duties and obligations of a government.

What is the first test of a government? It is to keep order at home, and then to deal honorably with foreign powers. Life and property are just as secure tonight in Petrograd and Moscow as in New York or Chicago. The laws of that country are as thoroughly enforced, so far as the protection of human life is concerned, as in any country in Europe. It is true they passed through the cruel, bloody period which characterizes revolution ever and always, for which no man would even attempt to make an apology. They passed through a period characteristic of all great revolutions, and there never has been a revolution upon such a stupendous scale as this; but at the present time and for months and months past they are meeting the supreme test of a government, and that is the protection of property and of life, notwithstanding the venal and corrupt propaganda which is constantly being sent out in this country.

To give you an idea, if I may turn to it hastily, about the manner in which this cause is repeatedly presented to us, Captain Estes, in making a speech a few nights ago in the city of New York before the Republican Club, stated, according to the press dispatch, as follows:

Capt. W. B. Estes, who was kept in a soviet jail in Moscow for a year during the World War, declared that to his certain knowledge there is in New York banks to the credit of the Lenin-Trotski government $540,000,-000.

He said:

New York banks held at least $180,000,000 in gold while I was locked up in jail, and the deposits are three times that sum now. The most of it is with Kuhn, Loeb & Co. and the Guaranty Trust Co., although many other banks have heavy deposits. Much of it is in old Russian gold rubles.

The intention undoubtedly was to disclose that Lenin and Trotski were not only tyrants but were also engaged in robbing their people, pushing their money out of the country which they were wrecking, so that in the hour of escape they would have something with which to take care of themselves. It has been repeatedly circulated over this country that this was true and that they were engaged not in an attempt, however unwisely from our viewpoint, to construct a government but in holding power for a sufficient length of time to enable them to take care of themselves financially in proper fashion. I thought, in view of the fact that Captain Estes had mentioned the firms, that we might indeed find out whether they had the money on hand. I telegraphed to these two banks as follows:

Are you free to state to me the facts concerning the statement of Captain Estes relative to Lenin-Trotski government having large deposits in your bank?

Kuhn, Loeb & Co. replied:

We are in receipt of your telegraphic inquiry. We have never had any dealing of any nature with the Lenin-Trotski government, and have no deposit, directly or indirectly, for their account.

The president of the Guaranty Trust Co. says:

I assume your telegram of today refers to Captain Estes's statement before the National Republican Club, as reported in Sunday's New York Tribune. We have no deposit here to the credit of the Soviet Government, either in gold or otherwise.

Comment is unnecessary. It is a fitting sample of the misinformation which the people in this country are given with reference to Russia. Countless other illustrations might be given. I do not know Captain Estes. I shall assume he was also misinformed. But it certainly seems the statement was without foundation.

Mr. President, let us review briefly, as nearly as we can from accurate statements, the actual present condition of affairs in Russia.

I shall ask, first, the privilege of reading a portion of a letter from Bishop Neulsen, of the Methodist Episcopal Church, who has been for many months in Russia, and, as I understand, is there now. This letter is addressed to me under date of December 8, 1922. Knowing that Bishop Nuelsen had been for a long time in Russia, and that his business was the occasion of his being there, and knowing something of the standing of Bishop Neulsen in the Methodist Church, it seemed to me that whatever his view might be it would be one upon which we could reasonably rely, especially as to those things which are open to observation. He says:

As far as I was able to observe, the present government in Russia is as firmly established as any government in Europe. I do not look for a revolution, but I do expect that a gradual evolution will take place. I did not find anybody in Russia who looked forward to a revolution, even among those who were quite outspoken in their criticism. One of the American newspaper correspondents whom I met in Moscow had just returned from a trip through the greater part of the country, and he said to me with reference to the government, "There is not a crack in sight."

The argument often presented to us is that this Government does not represent the Russian people at all, that it is a coterie of autocrats who have seized control of affairs, that the people of Russia as a people are not in sympathy with it, and that it does not represent them at all. That is not the view which Bishop Neulsen gets of the situation.

In fact, it is not the view which anyone would obtain who would make an impartial investigation, and there are good reasons for it. The peasantry constitute from eighty-five to ninety per cent of the people of Russia. They have been struggling for many, many decades to secure their land, and they have secured the lands under the present régime; not absolute title—and it is a very good thing they have not—but they have possession of the land and are availing themselves of the benefits of working the land and cropping the land just as completely as if the title were in them. The reason why the Russian peasantry were arrayed almost solidly against Denikin, Wrangle, and Kolchak was because they believed that the restoration of the old régime, or of anyone who represented the views of the old régime, would be to deprive them of their lands; and, while Bishop Neulsen says they expect the evolution of this government, the working out of a more satisfactory form of government, they are not in favor of destroying the present government or of accepting as leaders and as governors those who are opposed to this form of government. They prefer to work out their salvation upon the principle of evolution, as other peoples have to do who have changed their government from despotic forms to revolutionary forms of government. Therefore these people are thoroughly behind the government so far as it is opposed by other governments, whatever may be their view as to the necessity of reforming the government itself.

Again, Bishop Neulsen says:

In a public address in the city of Boston Bishop Neulsen said:

Whatever may be said, however, against the Soviet Government—and I would not condone its crimes and foolishness—it must be said that order is now being reestablished. One can move along the crowds in Petrograd and Moscow in perfect safety. The railroad furnishes good service, and the trains are on time.

* * * * * * * *

The Soviet Government has a department of education larger than any other department, and is making an honest effort to train the people. The equipment of the schools, however, is scant, there being almost no textbooks; but the teachers work with apparent enthusiasm and an earnest desire to educate the coming generation.

What is the attitude of the Soviet Government toward religion? I would reply that there is perfect liberty to preach.

Doubtless all who honor me with their presence will remember the attack which was made some time ago upon the Soviet Government because of its persecution of the church, and it was for that reason that I made particular inquiry of Bishop Neulsen in regard to it.

Suffice it to say that in my opinion there was no persecution of religion. There was prosecution, and, I would admit, if it were deemed essential, persecution of political agitators who were covering themselves under the cloak of religion, men who were opposing the present form of government, who were seeking to agitate against the Government and seeking to protect themselves under the cloak of religion in doing so; but not a persecution or prosecution of the church as such or of religion as such.

I have before me also an article by a commander in the American Navy, some few paragraphs of which I desire to read. He has been in Russia for the last two or three years and was there until a short time ago. He was there when Kolchak and Wrangel were carrying forward their plans for the seizure of the Russian Government. He said:

We have today the good will of the great mass of the Russian people, as no other nation has.

*　　*　　*　　*　　*　　*　　*　　*

It follows then that recognition based not on commercial interest or advantage but on a real regard for the interests of the Russian people will mean a still greater extension of that good will toward the American people—a by-product of a right action on our part to which we will be as clearly entitled as we were to the happy results of Lincoln's great policy toward the South.

* * * * * * * *

My own opinion is influenced very largely by another fact, which many people consider almost as irrevelent, but which to me is the deciding weight. It is that under the Soviet Government the Russian people have at last gotten what they have always demanded above all else; what even Czarist governments have promised them but have failed to accomplish; what all the leaders that have since arisen—Kolchak, Denikin, Wrangel—all have promised and all have failed to do; that is, under the Soviet Government the peasants have gotten the land. Under all other governments the peasants got only promises that were never kept.

* * * * * * * *

I have also a statement made by ex-Gov. James P. Goodrich, of Indiana, who, as we all know, has been very much in Russia for the last two years. He says:

Out of the present unfortunate situation a settled responsible government shall emerge. It will be a democracy and not an autocracy, either of the Czar or the proletariat. The peasant never did accept communism. He is by instinct, training, and tradition individualistic and capitalistic.

* * * * * * * *

One's life and liberty are as safe in Russia today as in any other country in Europe, provided always he is not perniciously active in politics. The process of evolution is still going on. When we get far enough away to write an impartial history we will marvel at the swiftness of the change rather than its slowness.

It seems, Mr. President, we have a government which has been in existence now for nearly six years, which, according to those who are certainly in a position to judge and impartially to report, has the support of the Russian people; a government which is maintaining law and order throughout Russia; a government which has withstood all attacks from without and from within; a government which put down three powerful invasions financed by outside powers; a government which has stood alone six years in Europe. It is the only government which came out of the war which could stand alone.

That being true, the next question is, What is the relationship of that government to the other governments? Is it prepared to deal in a way that the other governments can afford to recognize it and undertake to do business with it?

At the present time there are sixteen nations

trading with Russia, either through treaties or through agreements, either by reason of recognition or by reason of trade treaties or agreements. I do not know of a single instance in which it has been successfully charged that Russia has in any way disregarded these trade agreements. I recall, which perhaps may be in the minds of others, an instance in which it was charged that the Soviet Government disregarded one of the trade agreements. There has been a controversy about that by those who were beneficiaries of the agreement, one of the gentlemen contending that the government discharged its agreement as it was made, another contending that it disregarded it. But if that be an exception it is the only exception of which I have been able to learn in which there has been any charge of a break in the integrity of the contracts with reference to commercial relations between Russia and the governments which have trade agreements with it.

I wish now to refer to a dispatch which was printed in the New York Times on the 15th of the present month, a dispatch from Mr. Duranty. Neither the Times nor Mr. Duranty would be charged with conscious bias in favor of the Soviet Government. I assume that they would state the facts as they understood them, and would not be consciously biased in favor of that Government. The dispatch, under date of February 15, said:

Moscow, February 15—Foreigners can do a profitable business in Russia today. They are doing it already, and whereas a year ago foreign business men here were mostly represented by fly-by-night firms and were interested in highly speculative, not to say wildcat, transactions, today there are Americans, Germans, British, Scandinavians, and even Frenchmen with real money beside them here to look the ground over.

For the Government or, rather, governmental trading organizations of one kind or another, stick to their contracts, and life and property are as securely guarded and as safe as they would be in America. What is more, the Government organizations are willing to guarantee against loss in transit, although the projected system of State insurance has not yet been carried through. For instance, a foreigner here shipped bales of valuable goods to Germany of which one, worth about $25,000, was lost between Moscow and the Lettish frontier. On discovering his loss he went to the foreign trade monopoly bureau which had given him a permit to buy and ship goods. The bureau took the matter up with the railroad authorities, who admitted their liability, and within two weeks the foreigner received from the railroad a check on the State bank payable in foreign currency for the amount of the purchase money.

Naturally, during and after the period of the Revolution there was uncertainty, there was insecurity with reference to trade relations, not any greater, I apprehend, than would have been in any country where such a revolution was going on. It is true also that they changed the status of private property in Russia which gave additional ground for fear upon the part of traders from the outside. But it seems now beyond question, and it has so appeared for many months, that so far as the trade of foreign governments is concerned, a status is fixed which makes it safe and secure, that property rights are respected and protected, and that the Russian Government is prepared, so far as foreign powers are concerned, to disregard the principle of communism which obtains with reference to the internal affairs of Russia, although it obtains now only in limited degree.

Now, if it be true—and I have an abundance of other material here which I might submit—that a government is there established, doing business, protecting lives, protecting property, and respecting trade relations with other nations, it is not worth while for the United States to establish a friendly relation with those 140,000,000 of people? There can be no peace in Europe as long as Russia is an outlaw.

What is it that makes the Near East situation so full of menace today? It is because this great outlaw nation there, with her 140,000,000 people and with her vast man power, is coming in touch, by reason of the situation in which we have placed her, with the disciplining and organizing power of Germany. We risk much in war. We risk much when it comes to engaging in conflict. May we not risk something for the purpose of establishing friendly and amicable relations with these great powers in Europe?

What could we possibly lose? What would be the loss to the United States if we should recognize the government of Russia?

I can conceive of nothing which could be estimated as a loss, except that which they contend, that the business men of this country would not have their security and therefore might lose some material interests. But there are two answers to that. In the first place the business men of the country are willing to go into Russia and willing to take the risk, even without recognition. Certainly they would be more secure and safer with their government, our ambassador, and their consuls than they are without them. If there be anything to adjust with Russia or business relations to be strengthened, may we not do so better with our ambassador and consuls and dealing in a friendly way than through estrangement and with a stream of enmity flowing between us?

I have here a paper published under the head of the Amexa News. It is published by the American Manufacturers' Export Association, 160 Broadway, New York. I notice among its officers are Myron W. Robinson, of the Crex Carpet Co.; James A. Farrell, of the United States Steel Corporation; C. P. Coleman, of the Worthington Pump & Machine Corporation; H. J. Fuller, Fairbanks, Morse & Co., and so on, a body of men who are practical business men, to say nothing of anything else, would naturally look with a scrutinizing eye upon Russia or any other government where their property might be insecure or unsafe. There is a vast amount of material in this publication with reference to business conditions in Russia and the safety or the security which a person would have in doing business with the Russian people. I shall undertake to read but very little of it. Upon page 8 it is said:

The cooperative societies, like a network, cover every town, village, and hamlet throughout the wide, expansive territory of Russia and Siberia.

The cooperative societies passed unscathed through the revolution. They were undisturbed. They continued to do business, and they carried out their contracts both at home and abroad; and they are the basis of the industrial life of Russia at the present time.

The initial efforts of the movement proved such a phenomenal success that it rapidly spread throughout the country. It is a democratic institution, created and managed by the people to supply their needs and to foster their welfare. It was instigated by lofty ideals, but, contrary to most other organizations founded on such idealistic principles, it applied itself to its manifold tasks in a practical manner. An organization so constituted was certain to make rapid strides. It merits the remarkable success it has attained.

As the individual cooperative societies progressed they found that still further economies could be attained by the formation of provincial wholesale cooperative societies. Thus the individual cooperatives of the province of Astrakhan organized and became members of the Astrakhan Reginal Union of Consumers Societies, the cooperatives of Archangel organized and became members of Archangel Union of Cooperatives, and so on throughout the various provinces of the country.

On page 9 it is further said:

In the year of 1898 the All-Russian Central Union of Consumers Societies was established. It is commonly known both in Russia and abroad as centrosoyus—a contraction in the Russian language meaning central union. The centrosoyus is an organization consisting of all the provincial and individual cooperative societies in Russia and Siberia and might properly be termed a superwholesale cooperative society. All national and international activities of the cooperative societies are concentrated in this body. All imports into Russia and Siberia and exports from Russia and Siberia are handled by this organization. It has established banks, savings banks, insurance and credit societies, operates schools, libraries, hospitals, sanitariums, hotels, theaters, moving pictures, etc., for the benefit of its members.

It is a common belief in this country that all organizations now operating in Russia and Siberia are branches of the Soviet Government. While this may be true in a number of instances, it does not apply to the Centrosoyus. The Centrosoyus is a free and independent organization, which the government has seen fit to grant special privileges because of its altruistic ideals. In fact, the Centrosoyus is the only cooperative society in Russia and Siberia operating today, having replaced all other cooperative societies which previously existed separately. Direct trade with Russia and Siberia through those functions now existing outside of Russia and Siberia only, which have refused to reconcile themselves to the new order of affairs in Russia and Siberia, is now impossible.

It must be pointed out, however, that the Soviet Government exercises a certain measure of regulation over the Centrosoyus. Just as our Government or any other government exercises a certain measure of regulation over its nationals, so also the Soviet Government exercises the same degree of control over the Centrosoyus. The Centrosoyus is free to import such merchandise as the government tariff permits into Russia and Siberia unhampered and to export such products as are available to foreign countries. In fact, the government in many instances has encouraged them on in their foreign activities rather than to place obstacles in their path.

In the bulletin of the "All-Russian Central Union of Consumers Societies—Centrosoyus" dated September 15, 1922, the following paragraph appears, which would seem to indicate quite clearly the attitude of the government toward the Centrosoyus:

" * * * The Soviet Government is facilitating the work of the cooperation which is enjoying the position of 'maximum of preference.' One of the proofs of this is the granting by the government to the cooperatives of a 25 per cent reduction in the taxes levied for the State. * * * "

The centrosoyus, as far as their activities abroad are concerned, enjoy a spotless record, notwithstanding the fact that they have just emerged from a period of time during which they have been obliged to overcome those serious difficulties occasioned by the conditions in Russia. Their transactions in the foreign market, previous to the revolution, were on a considerable scale, and yet, notwithstanding the difficult period they have just passed through, they have never failed to meet a dollar's obligation to any foreign creditor.

This is from an article contributed to the publication by Mr. Valerian E. Greaves, who seems, as I understand, to have spent a great deal of time in Russia as the representative of some business interests.

Since the new economic policy was adopted—

That is, the policy which was announced by Lenin in March, 1921—

the latter repeatedly stated that private enterprise, domestic as well as foreign, was welcome in Soviet Russia, and that enterprisers' rights and interests will be fully protected.

* * * * * * * *

Just a word with reference to the Russian debt. I presume that one of the obstacles to the recognition of Russia has been what is supposed to be her unwillingness to recognize the old Czar debts. I can well understand, Mr. President, the hesitancy of the Russian people as a people to recognize those debts. It has been the firm policy of the Anglo-Saxon people always to treat the financial integrity of a country with the same consideration as one would individual integrity, and therefore nothing I say should be construed as a justification of any hesitancy upon the part of the Russian Government to recognize these debts. Nevertheless, one can well understand why it would be so when he considers the manner in which those debts were incurred.

Those debts were created largely for the purpose of building up a vast bureaucratic and military establishment in Russia, and were a part of the preparations which were going on in Europe for the deluge which came in 1914. However, Russia has signified her willingness to recognize those debts. She did it at Genoa; and I have not the slightest doubt that Russia, if she were recognized and given an opportunity and a position among the nations of the world, would carry out the suggestion which she made at Genoa and would recognize these debts; and I have no doubt but she would agree to pay them in sixty-two years. If such terms could be granted, from the statements which Tchitcherin and others who are in responsible position have made, I should not have any hesitancy in prophesying that those debts would be unhesitatingly recognized and taken care of. I will read just a line from Mr. Lloyd-George after he returned from Genoa:

That, roughly, is the position which they took with regard to debts—the money which had been advanced to Russia before the revolution. They were prepared to acknowledge those debts; they were prepared to make arrangements for their repayment.

As stated by Tchitcherin at Genoa, they could not well go home and say that they had recognized the debts of the Czar government, which was so very obnoxious to the Russian people, and at the same time say they had been refused recognition by the governments to whom they had recognized those debts. Suppose Mr. Lloyd-George or the representative of France had consented to any such absurd policy upon the part of their governments, their ministries would not have lasted until they got home. As Mr. Lloyd-George very well says, the Russian officers themselves had a situation to deal with at home. They could not any more disregard the public opinion of their country than the Congress of the United States would disregard the opinion of its constituents.

It was a very natural thing for the representatives of Russia to say at Genoa, "We are prepared to recognize these debts; we are prepared to make arrangements for their payment; we are prepared to settle all these matters provided we are given an opportunity which will afford any possibility at all of our carrying out our contract after we have recognized the debts."

Would we have been in any worse position if recognition had taken place a year ago or two years ago than we are at the present time? It is a speculation of course, and it is also a speculation as to the benefits which would have flowed. But what is the basis of recognition? Why do we recognize governments? To enable us to establish such friendly relations as that we may do business with other members of the family of nations so that we may adjust such matters as debts and commercial affairs and retain friendly relations with them.

Suppose the present Government of Russia fails, what then? Suppose that by reason of our failure to recognize Russia, the failure of France to recognize Russia, and the failure of Great Britain to recognize Russia—although quasi recognition has taken place in the case of Great Britain—the present Government of Russia fails and falls, what is there to take its place? What has the future in store for the Russian people in case the only semblance of authority now there disappears? Chaos, hopeless, unending misery, bloodshed, and possibly ultimately a reestablishment of some representative of the old régime. If the present Government of Russia fails, if it falls, and there is nothing to take its place in Russia except that which may come out of the turmoil which may follow and concerning which no man can prophesy, the misery which has already been registered in that country will be repeated

again, and even at the end of it who shall
prophesy that they will have anything better
than they have at the present time?

The present Russian Government has been
in existence for six years; it has gone through
the chaotic period; it is in the process of evolution; it represents authority; it represents at
the present time the support of the Russian
people. It is protecting life and property; it
is transacting business with foreign nations;
it is discharging every duty and obligation
which rests upon a government, whether it be
according to our idea of what a government
should be or not; and if by our connivance or
our failure to accord recognition it breaks
down, we shall necessarily as a moral proposition become responsible in a large degree for
what is to follow. Who is to take its place?
Semenoff, or some representative of Wrangel,
or some of the refugees whose interest in Russia is to see the old régime restored? In my
humble opinion, the Russian peasant will suffer incalculable misery and go through years
of turmoil before he will return to the old régime. Is it not infinitely better in a friendly
way to undertake to bring Russia to the
position which she ought to occupy under a
sane and sound democratic form of gov-

ernment? For myself, sir, I do not want
to see my Government connive at a policy which will add misery to that great
people, which may bring on years of civil
war, which may restore the old rule with all its
incompetency and corruption and cruelty.
Think for a moment what it all means. Let us
forget for a time a few individuals and think
of the mass of suffering humanity in case of
another revolution or counter-revolution, the
women and children who must pay with their
lives for the wickedness of such a course. We
are constantly saying officially we sympathize
with the people of Russia. Is it not time to
give evidence of that sympathy by deeds? * *

Let me digress to say that if it is true that
they are engaged or would continue to be engaged in propaganda which is designed to present their view of government to the people of
the United States, could we not more effectually deal with it if we were upon friendly relations with them than we can now? What possible reason would they have for continuing
an unfriendly act upon their part toward this
Government after amicable relations had been
established, and it was to every interest of the
Russian Government and the Russian people
to build up the friendliest relations and to ac-

centuate trade relations between the two Governments? They would have no occasion for continuing any such course; and in view of the fact that they have modified their communistic form of government entirely and completely from that which existed at the time the propaganda was going on, they would have no occasion, from the standpoint of an apostle, to continue the advocacy of such doctrines. * *

I never have been able to understand the shivering fear which some people in this country entertain with reference to the effect of this propaganda from Russia or elsewhere. Whom is it going to hurt? I do not think it would affect the Senate. I do not think it would affect the House of Representatives. Whom are you afraid of—the farmer? It is the farmer in Russia who has destroyed or modified communism. It is the peasantry in Russia that represents individualism. It is the eighty-five per cent of people of Russia who have made that propaganda absolutely worthless and futile. You could pile your carloads of propaganda into the center of the agricultural population of the country and they would use it for fuel. Whom is it going to undermine?

Let me tell you. If you will take the tax burdens off the people of this country, if you will restore economic conditions so that they may have an adequate price for their products, if you will lift the burden which is crushing the people of the world through militarism and through armaments, there will be very little soil in which to sow the seeds of Bolshevism. Our conduct toward Russia has fed Bolshevism from the beginning. It has strengthened Lenin and Trotski every day that it continued to exist, so I do not know what they would do; I do not care what they would do. I am perfectly willing to trust the American people against such propaganda. I do not know of any soil so sterile in which to sow and let die the seeds of Bolshevism as the common people of America. I will trust our people to deal with such propaganda.

Let us go back again to the Revolutionary period.

On the 18th day of April, 1793, Washington notified his Cabinet that they would have a Cabinet meeting the next day. On the 19th day of April, 1793, they had a Cabinet meeting. He notified them in the letter that the subject about which they would confer would be whether or not they should recognize the revolutionary government of France. They met upon the 19th; and let us look in upon the Cabinet meeting for a moment.

There was Washington, who was not only a great general but had some knowledge about building governments; Hamilton, who was in many respects the greatest constructive genius who ever dealt with the science of government; and Jefferson, the most wide-ranging political philosopher that the world has ever known. It was the greatest Cabinet that ever sat under the American flag, if not in the world. It was their business to know government. They did know it. It was their business to know the proper relationship between governments, and they did know it, as no other three men in the world who ever assembled at one time knew these things. There, upon the 19th day of April, 1793, in less than a two hours' conference, they unanimously voted to recognize the revolutionary government of France.

What was the revolutionary government of France at the time they recognized it? It consisted of what was known as the Committee of Public Safety, and nothing else. Every foot of property in France and every human life in France were under the control and at the disposal of what was known as the Committee of Public Safety. At its head at that time was

Danton, with him was Barrere, and later at its head was Robespierre, whose head it took off on the 28th of July, 1794.

This was the government which Washington and Hamilton and Jefferson recognized. I do not read in the account of that conference that they discussed what possible trade could be built up between France and the United States, or whether property or human life was safe in France. Only a short time before the recognition the King had been beheaded, and only a short time afterwards Marie Antoinette suffered death. The guillotine was running every morning. It was after this that the massacre took place in the prisons; and yet Washington, in his wisdom, supported by Hamilton and Jefferson, said: "These people are working out in their own way their salvation"; and so close were they to the days in which they had purchased their own liberty that they were willing to give the French people an opportunity to work it out in their own way. * * *

May I read a letter from Washington, addressed to a friend, found in that very valuable book by the Senate historian?

George Washington, in a letter written to a friend in regard to this matter, said:

My conduct in public and private life, as it relates to the important struggle (of the French Revolution) in which the latter (France) is engaged, has been uniform from the commencement of it, and may be summed up in a few words: That I have always wished well to the French Revolution—

That does not sound harsh or Bolshevik now, but think of how it must have grated upon the sensitive nerves of this gentleman who had criticized him at the time!

I have always wished well to the French Revolution.

Bloody and inhuman as it was, cruel and merciless as it was, he wished it well, because it was the process by which they chose to get rid of a government which was worse; and, bad as the Soviet Government may have been in its worst hours, it is infinitely better than the cruel and unspeakable history of the Czars for the last one hundred and fifty years.

That I have always wished well to the French Revolution; that I have always given it as my decided opinion that no nation has a right to intermeddle in the internal concerns of another; that everyone had a right to form and adopt whatever government they liked best to live under themselves.

And at the time he wrote this letter France was in a condition not better, Mr. President, and scarcely worse, I presume it will be said, too, than Russia in its most distressed period; but that time has passed now. That period has gone by, and order has come out of chaos, and we are in a very much more advantageous position from every standpoint to recognize Russia than Washington and Hamilton and Jefferson were upon the 19th of April, 1793, with reference to France.

May I read a single paragraph in description of the Government and the conditions in France at the time it was recognized? This is from Macaulay:

Then came those days when the most barbarous of all codes was administered by the most barbarous of all tribunals; when no man could greet his neighbors or say his prayers or dress his hair without danger of committing a capital crime; when spies lurked in every corner; when the guillotine was long and hard at work every morning; when the jails were filled as close as the hold of a slave ship; when the gutters ran foaming with blood into the Seine; when it was death to be great-niece of a captain of the royal guards or half brother of a doctor of the Sorbonne, to express a doubt whether assignats would not fall, to hint that the English had been victorious in the action of the 1st of June, to have a copy of one of Burke's pamphlets locked up in a desk, to laugh at Jacobin for taking the name of Cassius or Timoleon, or to call the Fifth Sans-culottide by its old superstitious name of St. Matthew's Day. While the daily wagon loads of victims were carried to their doom through the streets of Paris, the proconsuls whom the sovereign committee had sent forth to the departments reveled in an extravagance of cruelty unknown even in the capital. The knife of the deadly machine rose and fell too slow for their work of slaughter. Long rows of captives were mowed down with grapeshot. Holes were made in the bottom of crowded barges. Lyon was turned into a desert. At Arras even the cruel mercy of a speedy death was denied to the prisoners. All down the Loire, from Saumur to the sea, great flocks of crows and kites feasted on naked corpses twined together in hideous embraces. No mercy was shown to sex or age. The number of young lads and girls of 17 who were murdered by that execrable government is to be reckoned by hundreds. Babies torn from the breast were tossed from pike to pike along the Jacobin ranks. One champion of liberty had his pockets well stuffed with ears. Another swaggered about with the finger of a little child in his hat. A few months had sufficed to degrade France below the level of New Zealand.

Mr. President, the great statesmen of England who were then at the head of the English Government refused to follow the example of Washington and continued to discuss the question of whether England would recognize the so-called government of France, or treat with it, or in any way assume a relationship with the government of France such as would even imply recognition. Pitt and Fox continued to discuss the matter for many years after Washington had recognized the government of France.

What was the effect of the recognition, so

far as we were concerned? It immediately established a relationship between this Government and the authorities of France under which Washington was able to say to that government, "We do not like your representative, Mr. Genét, who is engaged in"—what we would call now propaganda—"seeking to undermine our theory of government," and upon the suggestion of Washington, Genét was displaced and another was sent in his place.

The so-called propaganda, which was then quite as rife in this country from France as it ever has been in this country from Russia, and even more so, was discontinued within a very short time after that recognition took place. The relationship which was established continued until it was broken by reason of another incident entirely.

Pitt and Fox continued to discuss the matter, and if Senators will take up Mr. Pitt's speech made upon the 3d day of February, 1800, they will find that the arguments at the present time against the recognition of Russia are nothing new in that regard. Every conceivable question which has been raised as to our recognition of Russia was raised by Pitt in relation to the proposed recognition by England of France. He said that France was an armed system, that it was not a Government at all, that it was irresponsible, that it did not protect property or life, that it would not respect treaties, that the people of England could have no protection against the inroads made by reason of the Jacobin clubs, which were being organized in England itself, and for that reason he argued with great power against dealing with the French Government.

Fox, who has the honor of having been voted down more times in the English House of Commons than any other great leader, opposed the view of Mr. Pitt, referred to the act of Washington, and plead with them to deal with the people who were seeking to establish a democratic form of government, but the contest continued until it finally ended, as we know, after some eight years of struggle, upon the battle field. * * *

The speech of February 3, 1800, was made after the first consul came into power.

In a late article Painlevé, the former Prime Minister of France, said:

So long as Russia is not restored to the cycle of nations there will be neither economic equilibrium nor security in Europe.

But to imagine that Europe can know any rest while ignoring Russia, or, in the expression of a diplomatist, "letting her stew in her own juice till further notice," is to put up a claim for a comfortable life in a house in which the whole of the wall is missing on the side most exposed to wind and weather.

The ex-Premier of Italy, Orlando, said:

It is impossible to conceive a normal European existence with a State with over a hundred million inhabitants segregated, and it is unthinkable that a peace treaty can have brought a definite settlement of Europe until it has been ratified and sincerely accepted by the authorized representatives of that State.

What is the situation in Europe today? Of course, no one would prophesy that another war is at hand; but it is not aside to say that Europe is in a state of turmoil from side to side, from sea to sea, and by reason of the policies which have continued to be urged there are being driven together the Russian people, the German people, and this morning it looks as if a third were to join—the Mohammedans.

I can not understand why it is not the part of wisdom, in view of the conditions which now confront us, to do the simple thing, perfectly in accord with American traditions, in accord with the best traditions of America, to draw as friendly a relationship between those powers and the United States as possible.

If by the recognition of Russia we can hold

our friendship and deal with her in a friendly way, it may be the means, possibly, by which the conditions which now threaten war can be averted. At any rate, why should the United States pursue a policy of enmity, of strife, of contention with a government and a people, which government is satisfactory to those people and which people are friendly to us?

I said a moment ago that we are willing to risk everything in regard to war. We build navies and organize armies, and we go to great expense because we believe in security; but there is another basis of security, in my judgment, more permanent than that of force, and that is a friendly relationship, if it can be arranged, between the nations, which means more to the security of a people than mere armies and navies.

What would be the effect tomorrow morning if it were known throughout the world that the United States had recognized Mexico and established friendly relations with that nation and brought back the sympathetic relation of all the people of South America to the United States? Secondly, that the United States had recognized Russia and established friendly relations with that nation? What would be the psychological effect upon the condition of turmoil which now tortures the human family? Is it not time for us to take some steps, to make some move, to bring back friendly relations among the nations?

XIX

RECOGNITION OF RUSSIA

(In the United States Senate, May 31, 1922.)

It is now near the end of the fourth year since the signing of the armistice which put an end to actual hostilities in the World War. The Genoa conference and its ignoble ending reminds us, however, that our peace is nothing but war carried on in a different way. All the old purposes and passions, the ancient animosities, the intolerance, the relentless bigotry, which characterize war were at Genoa and finally encompassed its failure. There was not in that conference—speaking of the conference as a whole—a single move or plan based upon true principles of reconstruction. Everything was conceived and carried out in the spirit of destruction and war. Although Europe, with its vast armies, its military alliances, its tax-ridden people, its hungry men and women, its crippled, its diseased, and its indescribable misery, was spread out before those assembled, this, and all this, was not sufficient to brace the conference to a single high and honorable

241

resolve. The world has had to witness in its bloody and treacherous past many international conclaves, but none ever met with such great responsibilities confronting it, and none ever adjourned with so little to its credit.

It must be apparent to everyone that a continuance of the policies which have characterized the dominant powers of Europe since the war will either end in another world conflict or, if not in actual war, bring about such a condition of retrogression as will engulf the masses of all nations in unending peonage. The people want peace. They want to go back to work. They want to trade with each other and respect and recognize each other. But they are held back, as it were, in a leash by the policies of their political masters—policies which they are neither permitted to approve or condemn. Never was there a time when so much was being said about democracy, about unity and cooperation, and never have the people had so little to say about these things, and all things which involve liberty and life.

We have had four years of actual war— bloody and remorseless war—leaving as a legacy a debt which it is difficult for the human mind to comprehend, leaving the sick, the diseased, the blind, and the insane in every community. We have now also had four years of hate and vengeance, four years devoted to punishment and destruction. Is it not time to risk something, to venture something, in the cause of a new era, of a new order, to accept the creed, the fundamental tenet of which is live and let live? Has tolerance no part or place in post-war politics? Is every act or move of the victor Governments to be gauged solely by the question of material advantage or gain—coal or oil? Are questions of human rights and human liberties to have no weight in making up or shaping our policies? Shall we absolutely refuse to recognize those whose form of government does not suit us or who have not something to give us in the way of advantage in matters of trade and barter? Will not recognition promote friendly relations, and may we not forego something of our views and risk something in the cause of greater amity and peace?

The Russian problem is conceded by all to be the key to a restored Europe, to a peaceful Europe. There can be no such thing as peace in Europe, or a normal condition of affairs, or disarmament, or relief from taxes and similar burdens until the Russian problem shall have been settled. That was made evident at every session of the Genoa conference. Only in proportion as they were able to deal with that subject were they able to hold sessions which seemed to have any vital motive or any ultimate purpose or object to be attained.

Not only does the Russian problem involve the prosperity of Europe but it is only less important to this country. We may pass tariff bills, but until Europe is restored and the markets of Europe again resume, we can not hope to enjoy the prosperity or the contentment in this country which we are entitled to enjoy. Until the markets of Europe shall have been opened, and the manufacturers of this country can find a market for their surplus products, it will be impossible for them to buy, as they would necessarily have to buy, of the farmer in order to insure his prosperity. While the tariff bill has its place in the consideration of affairs at this time, until there is a settlement of the European situation upon policies which permit of the return to the ordinary duties and obligations of peaceful citizenship, we can not hope to enjoy prosperity in this country. Until the markets of Europe are open and the people of Europe are buying our economic situation here will be unsatisfactory.

This is not the time, even if I were able to

do so, to recount the history of the Russian people. It is as fascinating a story as has been written in the history of the world. But I do call attention very briefly to the part which Russia played in the Great War. It is a telling and at times the most controlling and determining part; a fact which, it seems to me, we ought not wholly to overlook at this time. It will enable us, it occurs to me, to form more tolerant, wiser, and sounder views concerning those people.

Lloyd-George, in his speech before the House of Commons upon his return from Genoa, used this language:

The Russians are a gallant people, a loyal and patient people, a people capable of greater heights of unselfish devotion than almost any race in the world, as they demonstrated through the first two or three years of the Great War, when more particularly on one occasion they sacrificed themselves in order to save the Allies; but a people accustomed for generations to obey ruthless and relentless authority, and who, under the lash of despair, had been very formidable to their neighbors.

This tribute is not in excess of their deserts. At one time the Russian people mobilized 21,000,000 men in the Great War. In February, 1917, they had 14,000,000 men in arms, fighting over a front of 3,500 miles. They had arrayed against them at one time one-third of the entire German Army, two-thirds of the Austrian Army, the entire Hungarian Army, and two-thirds of the Turkish Army. They lost during the war 2,500,000 men upon the field of battle and between 3,000,000 and 3,500,-000 wounded. They had prisoners taken to the number of 2,000,000, 1,000,000 of whom died in prison. They themselves captured some 400,-000 German prisoners, 1,000,000 Austrians, and 300,000 Hungarians. Indeed, as the Premier of England said, at one time they sacrificed themselves in order to save the Allies.

No nation suffered more or sacrificed more in the Great War during those years than the Russian people, and the fighting which they did was never excelled on any front in the world struggle or elsewhere. As has been recounted before, being without arms, in a large measure deprived of the means of carrying on the conflict which they should have had, they stood beside their fighting comrades, seized weapons from the falling men, and continued the battle. Indeed, it is said that at times they fought the opposing forces with their bare fists. Those are matters which ought to throw some light upon what we may expect of the Russian people, as a people, when they are given an opportunity to demonstrate the qualities they actually possess.

During the war came the revolution in Russia. It has had the course of all great revolutions. It came rather unexpectedly, even among the Russian people. It took a course in some respects wholly unexpected. Indeed, human foresight can not foresee or gauge the course of these great mass movements, these revolutions which shake continents. There is no law, human or divine, by which to judge them. They are a law unto themselves. In defiance of all preconceived plans or mortal schemes they set up their own standards and map out, even as they move, their own course. Eccentric, unnatural, remorseless, some blind, inherent force seems to drive them along their bloody pathway in utter disregard of the purposes of their instigators, and exempt from all control of their supposed masters. Their end and their results no one can foresee.

The final results are often beyond all anticipation, even of their most powerful actors. If there be in human affairs such a thing as fate, imperious and inexplicable, master of the human will, transcendent over the human intellect, it is most manifest in these upheavals of human passion. We see crimes committed, with no apparent object in view; cruelty, senseless and purposeless, practiced; deeds done to the utter confusion of the perpetrators; policies, ruthless and self-destructive, urged and pursued; and yet, in the end a result obtains conducive to human progress, vital to the welfare of the human family and outweighing in good all the deplorable sacrifices by which it was achieved. In spite of all, the fateful drama goes forward, sinister and revolting figures cross and recross the stage, scenes close and the curtains fall, chaos seems to rule supreme; nevertheless, out of this woof and warp of crime and incompetency a higher life, a better people, a nobler nation, emerges. This was notably true as to the French Revolution, and I doubt not at all will be true of the Russian Revolution. In common with all who deplore human suffering and execrate those who inflict cruelty upon their fellows, I would prefer that these great changes could come about in a different way. Nevertheless, the change must come—it is a part of the law of human progress, the reason for which I am little able to understand and the justice of which it seems utterly useless to question.

One striking feature of this great movement which ought not to be overlooked, because it has had a very marked effect upon the attitude of mind of the Russian people, is that from the beginning the Allies expressed little sympathy with the revolutionary movement in Russia. With the exception of the United States, as those views were expressed by President Wilson, there was no true sympathy upon the part of the governments engaged in the war. Every move that was made seemed to have for its purpose the augmenting and sustaining of counter revolutions and, as a very great Russian has said, while the Allies seemed anxious to have Russia back in the war, there was little expression of feeling as to what the ultimate result of the struggle for free government in Russia should be.

As I have said, there was an exception to that in the expression made by this country through President Wilson, and, if I may, I take a moment to read the statement by the ex-President in his address to the Congress on January 8, 1918, in stating the war aims:

The evacuation of all Russian territories and a settlement of all Russian questions such as to insure the best and most untrammeled cooperation of other nations of the world in order to afford Russia a clear and precise opportunity for the independent settlement of her autonomous political development and of her national policy, promising her a cordial welcome in the League of Nations under institutions of her own choice, and besides a cordial welcome, help and assistance in all that she may need and require. The treatment meted out to Russia by the sister nations in the months to come must be a decisive proof of their good will, of their understanding of her needs as apart from their own interests and of their intelligent and disinterested sympathy.

That was, it seems to me, the true principle "under institutions of her own choice," sound and ancient American doctrine. "Afford Russia a clear and precise opportunity for independent settlement of her autonomous political development." Wiser words in regard to Russia have not been spoken. These were spoken January 8, 1918, long after the fall of Kerensky and the advent of Lenin.

The expression of that view at that time was received throughout Russia with approval, and undoubtedly created a feeling of confidence in the American policy. It is one of the unfortunate things of the war, one of the things which has left disaster and suffering in its wake, that that policy in the first instance expressed has not been undeviatingly pursued by the Government of the United States. We had nothing to gain by deviating from the most sympathetic and helpful policy toward the Russian people, and we had everything to lose by adopting a different course.

There has been in history, so far as I know, but one revolution to be compared with the Russian Revolution, and I want to draw some comparisons today between the French Revolution and the Russian Revolution. I want to look in upon the French Revolution during its progress, observe the issues and the principles which were raised, the questions which were presented to the outside nations, and the manner in which outside nations dealt with the subject in hand. It seems to me it establishes a precedent to which we may recur, if not for absolute guidance, yet for wise suggestion as to the present situation.

There is scarcely a principle or a proposition which has been raised by outside nations with reference to the Russian Revolution which was not raised and presented and discussed and considered and determined by outside nations with reference to the French Revolution. There was scarcely a question of policy considered at that time different from that which has been presented with reference to the Russian Revolution. I am going to recur briefly, in order to secure a better statement of those issues than I can present, to the great debate between Pitt and Fox relative to what England should do in the matter of treating and trading with the French Republic and with reference to its recognition.

We should bear in mind that for twelve long years two of the ablest statesmen of the English-speaking tongue discussed the policy of England with reference to the French Revolution. Then I want you to go with me to the policy which was adopted by our own Government under the leadership of men equally distinguished in statesmanship and, to my mind, much wiser in the policy which they adopted.

We are told in these days that nothing has ever occurred like the Russian Revolution in its atrocity, its inhumanity, and its cruelties, and nothing like the questions presented by it have ever before been presented. As we go through this debate, I invite attention to the fact that the things which we are discussing now are the things which they discussed in those days.

Mr. Pitt said in the famous debate on February 3, 1800:

I consider the French Revolution as the severest trial which the visitation of Providence has ever afflicted upon the nations of the earth.

This debate was taking place during the question of treating and trading with the Government of France, Mr. Pitt urging that the system which they had set up was in contravention to all orderly governments, that it had utter disregard for the sanctity of property or for the sacredness of life, and that the people who were at the head of it could not be trusted, and for England to recognize such a system of so-called government was to encourage the spread of the doctrines which they were teaching, which would result ultimately in the destruction of all orderly forms of government.

Upon page 98, of volume 3 of these debates, it is said:

They—

The French Republic—

had issued a universal declaration of war against all the thrones of Europe; and they had, by their conduct, applied it particularly and specifically to you—:

That is, the English Government.

They had passed the decree of the 19th of November, 1792, proclaiming the promise of French succor to all nations who should manifest a wish to become free; they had by all their language, as well as their example, shown what they understood to be freedom; they had sealed their principles by the deposition of their sovereign; they had applied them to England by inviting and encouraging the addresses of those seditious and traitorous societies who from the beginning favored their views, and who, en-

couraged by your forbearance, were even then publicly
avowing French doctrines and anticipating their success in
this country; who were hailing the progress of those proceedings in France, which led to the murder of its King;
they were even then looking to the day when they should
behold a national convention in England formed upon
simliar principles.

How similar to the fear of the spread of the
soviet doctrine into this country at the present
time. One of the main arguments against recognizing the soviet government is that this
would accentuate and tend to spread and to
some extent honor the doctrine which they say
is inimical to all forms of order and orderly
government.

Again, he said:

What would have been the effect of admitting this explanation? To suffer a nation, an armed nation, to preach
to the inhabitants of all the countries in the world that
themselves were slaves—

That is, the inhabitants of the other countries—

and their rulers tyrants; to encourage and invite them to
revolution, by a previous promise of French support, to
whatever might call itself a majority, or to whatever
France might declare to be so. This was their explanation;
and this, they told you, was their ultimatum.

This was the view of Mr. Pitt relative to
what he called an "armed system," not a gov-

ernment, not a responsible political entity, but an armed system controlled and directed by men who had no regard for property, for life, or for established order.

Upon page 105 it is said:

These terms should be—

That is, these are the terms which it was proposed should be made to France—

That these terms should be the withdrawing their arms within the limits of the French territory; the abandoning their conquests; the rescinding any acts injurious to the sovereignity or rights of any other nations; and the giving in some public and unequivocal manner a pledge of their intention no longer to forment troubles or to exite disturbances against other Governments.

Very similar, indeed, to the request which the Premier of England thought essential, and the idea which seems to be uppermost in the mind of the Government at Washington, a request which seems to be understood as necessary to be granted before any recognition of the soviet government can be had.

I call attention to this that we may understand that these questions have been met, and met by American leaders and American statesmen, as we shall see in a few moments. Before I go to that I want to read a paragraph or two in the reply from Mr. Fox. The reply was made on the same evening, and to my mind the greatest piece of debating of which history gives a record.

Fox, who was contending for the recognition of the French Republic and for treating and trading with the French Republic, said:

Gracious God! Were we not told, five years ago, that France was not only on the brink but that she was actually in the gulf of bankruptcy? Were we not told, as an unanswerable argument against treating, that she could not hold out another campaign; that nothing but peace could save her; that she wanted only time to recruit her exhausted finances; that to grant her repose was to grant her the means of again molesting this country; and that we had nothing to do but persevere for a short time, in order to save ourselves forever from the consequences of her ambition and her Jacobinism? What! After having gone on from year to year upon assurances like these, and after having seen the repeated refutations of every prediction, are we again to be seriously told that we have the same prospect of success on the same identical grounds?

For five years there has appeared in a large portion of the press of this country and from the lips of high officials the statement that within thirty days or sixty days, or at most within a brief period, the soviet government would collapse; that all we had to do was persist in the policy of non-recognition or non-aid, either one way or the other, and it must inevitably follow. For five years the soviet government has been meeting every test which can be applied to a government from without and from within. At the present time it seems to be conceded upon all hands that it is much stronger than it has been at any time during those five years. Notwithstanding that fact, the prophecy is still put forth—for the consolation of those, I suppose, who put it forth—that within a short time the soviet government is to fail, and to recognize it is to aid in its maintenance a little longer.

Further on Mr. Fox said:

Look back to the proclamations with which they set out. Read the declarations which they made themselves to justify their appeal to arms. They did not pretend to fear their ambition, their conquests, their troubling their neighbors; but they accused them of new modeling their own Government. They said nothing of their aggressions abroad; they spoke only of their clubs and societies at Paris.

Sir, in all this, I am not justifying the French—I am not striving to absolve them from blame, either in their internal or external policy.

Again he said:

I therefore contend, that as we never scrupled to treat with the princes of the house of Bourbon on account of their rapacity, their thirst of conquest, their violation of treaties, their perfidy, and their restless spirit, so we ought not to refuse to treat with their republican imitators.

When the whole story of all the cruelties and the atrocities of the soviet government shall have been told, it will not exceed or excel in brutality, in inhumanity, in cruelty those of a government which we have recognized ever since we have been in existence. My friend, the able Senator from New Jersey [Mr. Edge], said the other day that to recognize the soviet government with its present policies would be infamous. We recognized the czar's government at a time when the peasantry of Russia was tied to the land, whipped and sold and treated as common chattels. Is there anything in the present situation more infamous, more intolerable? Human language is inadequate to tell the story of the wrongs which have been heaped upon the peasantry of Russia these three hundred years—who said during these years we should withdraw recognition of Russia? It is said that we should not recognize Russia because the rights of property are not respected. Did we not recognize the old government when life was not respected; when human beings were ranked in dignity with the land?

Further on he said:

No man regrets, sir, more than I do the enormities that France has committted; but how do they bear upon the

question as it now stands? Are we forever to deprive ourselves of the benefits of peace because France has per-
petrated acts of injustice?

Now we come to the doctrine upon which
America proceeded, although this is stated by
Mr. Fox. Said Fox:

I think the people of France, as well as every other
people, ought to have the government which they like best
themselves; and the form of that government, or the
persons who hold it in their hands, should never be an
obstacle with me to treat with the nation of peace, or to
live with them in amity.

Let us turn now from the great debate between two great English statesmen, which continued off and on for twelve years. During its
continuance there continued war, conflict, the
sacrifice of human life, and continued deepening misery. Upon this side of the water the
same question arose as to whether or not we
should recognize the Republic of France.

I invite the attention of those who profoundly respect the Father of Our Country and the
Cabinet which surrounded him to some of the
views which they expressed, the action which
they took, and the result of policies which they
pursued. Upon the 18th day of April, 1793,
seven years prior to the debate when Pitt and
Fox were still discussing the question, Presi-

dent Washington sent a letter to Mr. Hamilton, and, as I remember, to all other members of the Cabinet, and in that letter was this question:

Question 2. Shall a minister from the Republic of France be received?

Question 3. If received, shall it be absolutely or with qualifications; and, if with qualifications, of what kind?

That, Mr. President, was on the 18th day of April, 1793. On the 6th day of April, 1793, there was established in Paris what was known as the Committee of Public Safety, twelve days before the writing of this Cabinet letter. That Committee of Public Safety held within its control and its unlimited discretion the life of every man, woman, and child within the confines of France. At the head of that Committee of Public Safety was Barere, of whom Macaulay could say he "tasted blood and felt no loathing; he tasted it again and liked it well." But the dominant and controlling figure of that committee was Danton. That committee was without law save the discretion of those who sat—nine of them—and the property and the lives and the destiny of France were absolutely within its control. The power of Lenin could not be greater, nor more arbitrarily or cruelly used.

What happened? This letter was sent out on the 18th day of April, 1793. On the 19th day of April, 1793, the Cabinet met and they unanimously decided to receive the minister from the French Republic. There was no dissenting voice among the members of the Cabinet. Shortly thereafter, on the 18th of May, 1793, Washington recognized Genet as minister of the French Republic in pursuance of the policy which had been outlined at a Cabinet meeting and agreed to unanimously by the Cabinet.

I call attention to the fact that this recognition took place at a time when I have said that Barere and Danton were at the head of the Committee of Public Safety. They continued until the 6th day of April, 1794, a year to a day subsequent. Upon the 6th day of April, 1794, Robespierre recognized the Committee of Public Safety and became its controlling spirit; and there has not been in all the history of the world such austere depravity as characterized the reign of terror under the last months of Danton and until the 28th day of July, 1794, when Robespierre died under the guillotine which he himself had been using in such a marked and ruthless way. During that time the wise, the farseeing Washington continued to recognize the French Republic.

Let us ascertain, if we can, upon what principles Washington and his Cabinet acted. However, before I proceed to that I will go a little further into some of the details of the organization of the French Republic during those days. On June 20, 1789, the representatives of France, finding the great hall closed, adjourned to the tennis court, and there took solemn oath that they would not adjourn until France should have a new constitution. If any particular and single event may be considered as the beginning of the French Revolution, I presume this might be so considered.

On July 14, 1789, the Bastille fell and the mob took control of Paris. In August, 1789, the assembly issued its declaration of the rights of man, which was a general statement of principles and the basis of civil society. The declaration of rights as made at that time was just as obnoxious, quite as much despised, and quite as much feared by the established order which then prevailed in Europe as is any enunciation which has come from the soviet government. It was regarded as inimical to all forms of government. Men were sent to prison in England for even advocating it; much more would they have been punished for practicing it.

In August, 1789, the assembly abolished all orders of nobility—the peerage, hereditary distinctions of all kinds and prerogatives of all kinds. On January 17, 1790, the Jacobin Club became the real political power in Paris and throughout France. It was a case of mob rule for a time.

In June, 1790, France was geographically redistricted and rearranged; her whole judicial system was revised; the power of the National Assembly was enlarged; church lands were confiscated; and all the old landmarks of government were obliterated. The guillotine was set up, and daily did its bloody work, and hundreds were executed.

In June, 1791, the King and Queen undertook to escape from France; were captured and brought back, and thereafter to all practical purposes were prisoners. On April 20, 1792, France declared war on Austria, and the long wars growing out of the French Republic began. Belgium was shortly thereafter invaded. On June 20, 1792, the mobs of Paris overawed the assembly and forced their way into the King's palace.

On August 10, 1792, Danton, at the head of

a vast mob, swept over the assembly and the monarchy, overpowering everything. The streets of Paris ran red with blood, and other cities were laid bare to the mob. About this time took place what is known as the fearful massacre of the prisoners in the different jails. On September 21, 1792, the convention abolished royalty and proclaimed a Republic. In November, 1792, began the trial of the King and shortly thereafter of the Queen. On November 19, 1792, the French Assembly issued what Pitt called a universal declaration of war, of which we have read in his speeches. On December 15, 1792, they issued another general proclamation of the same nature, declaring that the French Army would go to the assistance of all peoples who wished to abolish their governments and establish governments in harmony with the principles of the French Republic. On January 21, 1793, Louis XVI was executed, and thus the revolution threw down the glove to all Europe. On October 16, 1793, the Queen was executed. So within three months after execution of the King and prior to the execution of the Queen, Washington and his compeers saw fit to recognize the existence of the French Republic. Between the time of the execution of the King and the execution of the Queen occurred what was known in France as the reign of terror or mob rule. No language, Mr. President, which has been used, or which could be used in the description of the atrocities of the soviet government could exceed the atrocities which were practiced during those months. There must have been a deep, a profound reason for the recognition of that Government in France, to which we will come in a few moments.

On June 2, 1793, Lyons, by decree of the convention, was doomed to destruction; its name was to be blotted out; 3,500 were arrested, and half of them thrown into prison and massacred. Toulon and Marsailles suffered likewise. This was the condition in France at the time of the action of Washington's Cabinet.

Now, who composed that Cabinet? Excepting always, of course, living Cabinets, it was undoubtedly the greatest in all history, not only of our country but of all the world. They were not only administrators but they were builders of government; they were constructors; they were the carpenters who set up the fabric. There have not been in the history of mankind two men who better understood the science of government than Alexander Hamilton and Thomas Jefferson. The wide-ranging genius of Jefferson surveyed every possible activity within the political world, and Hamilton's constructive genius has never been excelled in the history of mankind. With them sat Washington, and these men, none of them in sympathy with the things which were being practiced in France, for reasons of peace, of stability, and the fundamental principle that a people have the right to set up their own government, recognized the existence of the French Republic and continued to do business with it from the 18th day of May, 1793 on, and the relationship was never broken.

I digress to quote a few words from Alexander Hamilton upon the French Revolution. It is one of the arguments, or rather one of the statements, made by those opposed to the recognition of soviet Russia that all who favor it are Bolsheviks and more or less in sympathy with the practices which have prevailed in Russia. I presume the same arguments would have been made in that day against Hamilton and Jefferson had there been living at that time those with such barren processes of thinking as seem to prevail upon the part of those who put forth these assertions now. Of course those who make such assertions well know them to be false, but falsehood is the handy weapon of the intellectual bankrupt.

Hamilton said, speaking of the French Revolution:

A league has at length been cemented between the apostles and disciples of irreligion and of anarchy. * * * The practical development of this pernicious system has been seen in France. It has seemed as an engine to subvert all her ancient institutions, civil and religious, with all the checks that seemed to mitigate the rigor of authority; it has hurried her headlong through a rapid succession of dreadful revolutions which have laid waste property, made havoc among the arts, overthrown cities, desolated provinces, unpeopled regions, crimsoned her soil with blood, and deluged it in crime, poverty, and wretchedness; and all this as yet for no better purpose than to erect on the ruins of former things a despotism unlimited and uncontrolled, leaving to a deluded, an abused, a plundered, a scourged, and an oppressed people not even the shadow of liberty to console them for a long train of substantial misfortunes, of bitter suffering.

George Washington, in a letter written later, quoting from page 140 of Lodge's Life of Washington, says:

My conduct in public and private life, as it relates to the important struggle [of the French Revolution] in which the latter [France] is engaged, has been uniform from the commencement of it, and may be summed up in a few words: That I have always wished well to the French Revolution; that I have always given it as my decided opinion that no nation has a right to intermeddle in the internal concerns of another; that every one had a right to form and adopt whatever government they liked best to live under themselves.

Notwithstanding the conditions which prevailed in France—the confiscation of property, the disregard of established institutions, the repudiation of debts, and the atrocities which were practiced—Washington was not willing to deviate from the proposition that a people have the right to set up whatever form of government they wish to live under and that it is the business of outside nations to recognize whatever form of government they may themselves see fit to establish. He talked little or not at all of trade, of safety of investments, of Bourbon debts—these matters he wisely supposed could be better handled after cordial relations were established. Time proved he was correct in his view. It was upon the basis of this policy, and in due regard for these principles, that the wise men sitting about the Cabinet table in 1793 concluded to recognize the French Republic. What was the result of it? Instead of the propaganda going forward in this country which seems to have been feared then from some sources, and is now feared with reference to Soviet Russia, it ceased almost entirely. The American Republic was a friend to the French people. There was no occasion to continue acts of enmity to our institutions or disregard of our wishes. The policy which Washington pointed out in 1793 and established was the policy to which England had to come, and to which Pitt, supported by Fox, had to accede after they had brought Europe to turmoil and destruction and war for fifteen long years.

Who can doubt in the light of history that had it been within the mind of Pitt to have accepted the policy of the wise leader of the western Republic the great war between France and England would have terminated ten years before it did? And just so surely as the policy which is now being pursued is pursued with reference to Soviet Russia it will inevitably continue and prolong the misery, the turmoil, and the discontent of Europe.

It may be possible, by reason of the policies which are being pursued, to break down the soviet government. It may be possible that it will fall. I do not pretend to say that it will not. But suppose the soviet government falls. What then? What takes its place? Here are 170,000,000 people in distress and in turmoil. There is only one directing force in it, and, as

Lloyd-George said at Genoa, there they sit, representing this 170,000,000 people. Suppose we destroy it, break it down, and plant chaos in the midst of Russia. What then? What government takes its place? What power will control and bring order? Who will speak to the warring forces and say: "Be still"? Are we willing to break down the only semblance of authority, the only semblance of order, which prevails in that country and leave it to utter chaos? What do we propose to give them instead? Shall we hunt out some representative of the old régime and force him upon the Russians? That would be infamous. Or shall we connive at the destruction of their present government and leave them to bloody chaos?

This is, as I might say, preliminary to the discussion of the practical questions, the vital questions, which will necessarily arise in connection with recognition. I am not going today to undertake to discuss them, but shall do so very shortly. I wanted to say this much as a preliminary to the discussion of the more practical propositions. There is the practical proposition of commercial relations, debts, and property. I shall discuss those things, I hope, very soon. I want to say in closing that I

make no concealment of the fact that I have
sympathized from the beginning with the revolutionary movement in Russia. I expressed
that opinion early in 1917, and I entertain the
same feeling now.

No people, with whose history I am familiar,
had been scourged and tortured as the Russian
people. They had suffered much and they suffered long at the hands of their corrupt and
merciless masters. The unrelenting and san-
guinary rule of the Romanoffs has no parallel
in all the annals of crime. If ever a people had
ample justification for overthrowing their government and seeking surcease of sorrow in a
new life, these people were more than justified.
The Great War, destroying, as it did, the root-
ed institutions of centuries also broke some fetters. In Russia, at least, they heard and believed that this war was being fought in the
interest of the people, of democratic government. With this gospel of a new life ringing
in their ears, the tragic year of 1917 was ush-
ered in. It found the whole social and economic fabric of Russia in collapse; a court mildewed
with the stupid superstitions and loathsome
lechery of Rasputin; venal public ministers
bartering their influence in the highest market;
millions cold and hungry in the streets with

bacchanalian debauchery in the places of power. Then came the breaking up of the great deep.

The elemental forces of human nature, crazed with hunger, wild with the hope of liberty, were released and the Russian Revolution was born. The reign of the Romanoffs was in any event to have an end. In that stupendous fact certainly all lovers of humanity may rejoice. The manner of their going, could it have been controlled, all would have been different, but that this dynasty should end once and for all is one of the compensations of the war. It had cursed and encumbered the earth long enough. And those who believe as I do in that kind of human progress which is initiated and sustained, not alone by great personages or dominant figures, nor guided by select groups of men, but which comes forward by reason of the great dumb forces of oppressed and outraged and downtrodden humanity, still believe that "the judgments of the Lord are true and righteous altogether."

Some will say such reasoning is to approve and commend these things done in the name of revolution. You might as well charge me with approving the atrocities of the French Revolution because I believe such revolution was unavoidable, that it marked the beginning of a new and far better era in France. I do not regret the Russian Revolution, but I do deplore its cruelties. Humanity seems sometimes to get into a trap from which there is no escape except to hew its way out. I regret the method, but I would not have humanity eternally entrapped. In these great social upheavals kings and lords and leaders are of but little concern and criticism is of no avail. The people are patient and long suffering before they are cruel. I do not know of a revolution in all history, a revolution which had its roots deep down in the sufferings and the sorrows and sacrifices of the people, but was amply justified and in the end altogether for the betterment and the advancement of mankind. I venture to believe the Russian Revolution will be no exception. In the end there will emerge a freer, a more released, a more democratic Russia. Untrained in the affairs of self-government, untutored in the duties and obligations of a free people, schooled alone by three hundred years of oppression and venal mastery, they are nevertheless a great people, a patient, kindly people, and from this fearful ordeal they will come forth a peaceful, home-loving, and self-governing people.

Ever since the Russian soldier carried back from France in the Napoleonic wars the seeds of democracy, a higher conception of liberty, there has been among them an unquenchable desire, an unconquerable purpose to be unchained and free. Now, belated but inevitable and upon the most stupendous and bewildering scale ever presented to the consideration of mankind, through blood and travail, through unspeakable suffering and infinite misery, they are working out their salvation. I make no apology for the awful mistakes committed on the way, but in the words of the leader of our own revolution, the father of our own country, I take the liberty to say:

Born in a land of liberty, my anxious recollections, my sympathetic feelings, my best wishes are irresistibly excited whensoever in any country I see an oppressed nation unfold the banners of freedom.

I believe the recognition of the de facto government of Russia would be in the interests of world peace, of the economic rehabilitation of Europe, and of the ultimate triumph of democracy throughout Russia. It would also be in harmony with the best traditions of our Republic and the high precedent established by one whose poise no political storm could disturb and whose intellectual vision neither political bigotry nor personal prejudices could cloud.

I am going to close my remarks by a quotation from Mr. Root when he was in Russia as a representative of this Government. In an address to the Russian provisional government Mr. Root said:

As we look across the sea we distinguish no party, no class. We see great Russia, as a whole, as one mighty, striving, aspiring democracy. We know the self-control, essential kindness, strong common sense, courage, and noble idealism of the Russian character. We have faith in you all. We pray for God's blessing upon you all. We believe you will solve your problems, that you will march side by side in the triumphant progress of democracy until the old order everywhere has passed away and the world is free.

Why can we not live up to that doctrine? Shall we forever pay lip service only to the great principles of humanity, to the great truths of international amity? I care less for the teachings and the doctrine now prevailing to some extent in Russia than many who decry them most. My ideal of government is that of a government of law—orderly, regulated liberty. I care nothing for theories or doctrines over there; I see only 170,000,000 Russian people, a great people, ultimately to be a powerful people, struggling in almost blinded madness to be free of the inhumanities and the cruelties of the past. It is with those people as a people that we should sympathize, and of them as a people we should think when forming our policies and mapping out our program. To say that the people do not want the present government of Russia is not borne out by the facts. It has stood for five years against conspiracies from within and conspiracies from without. The people have fought and sacrificed for it because they believed that it is the way to a better government and a freer democracy. It is their government. It is better for the world, better for peace, better for humanity, and better for the Russians that we recognize it and seek through friendly intercourse to modify those provisions which conflict not only with their interests but, as we believe, with the interests of all nations.

XX

POLITICAL PRISONERS

(Speech at Lexington Theater, New York, March 11, 1923.)

(Note: Mr. Borah and Mr. Pepper of Pennsylvania were Senate leaders in the movement for post-war tolerance. At the time of writing it is predicted that President Coolidge will soon grant to all the prisoners unconditional pardons.)

Ladies and Gentlemen: I am greatly pleased to have the opportunity of meeting so many of my fellow citizens for the purpose of considering and discussing what I believe to be a matter of extraordinary concern to the American people. There is involved in this discussion and the action which we seek upon the part of our government, not only the liberty of some fifty odd individuals, but broad and vital principles of free government.

During the Great War the Congress passed what is known as the Espionage Act. It was passed as a war measure. It was claimed that we had authority to pass it because we were engaged in war. I did not myself believe that even though we were engaged in war we had the power to pass the law, or perhaps I should say some of the provisions contained in the law, but I accredit to those who supported it

and voted for it the very best of motives. I
am, of course, not going today to engage in
a criticism of its passage. It was in war time.
We did that as we did many other things under
the stress and passion of war and believing it
was for the best interests of the country. But
that measure has now been taken from the
statute books. It was regarded as so obnoxious to the principles of free government that
shortly after the cessation of hostilities, the
agitation began for its repeal and it was finally
repealed as to the provisions with which we
are today concerned. It was not thought a fit
law to remain upon the statute books of the
United States in time of peace. It was believed that it interfered with that freedom of
action upon the part of the citizen which is
guaranteed by the fundamental principles of
our common Charter.

And so this law was taken off our statute
books and is now a thing of the past. I have
only one observation to make in regard to the
law, it being now repealed and that is, I trust
that at no time in the future will it ever be regarded or considered as a precedent for the
enactment of any measure of that kind again.
It should be regarded, in my opinion, as not
only opposed to the principles of free govern-

ment in time of peace but also in time of war. (Applause.) I do not believe that laws of repression, laws which deny the right to discuss political questions, are any more necessary in time of war than in time of peace and I do not believe they are constitutional either in time of war or in time of peace. (Applause.)

If this blessed old Republic cannot rest upon the free and voluntary support and affection of the American people in time of war as well as in time of peace, if we cannot, as a people, be free to discuss the political problems which involve limb and life, even in time of war, our government rests upon a very brittle foundation indeed. (Applause.)

But while the law has been repealed, the men who were sentenced under the law or a number of them, are still in prison. Four years have come and gone since the signing of the Armistice. Many months have passed since the repeal of the law. Still some fifty odd men are in prison under a law which we believed to be too obnoxious to the sense of American freedom and justice to remain upon the statute books. Certainly the dictates of humanity and the plainest principles of justice would demand that the men be given their freedom in any event from the time we repealed the law. (Applause.)

Many other governments had to deal with political prisoners. They had their political prisoners during the time that the war was in progress, but they all thought it just and wise immediately after the cessation of hostilities to release them. No other government engaged in the war has for the last three years had political prisoners. They have all been released, either through amnesty pardon, or by reason of the fact that their sentences being very short long since expired.

And so, my friends this Sunday afternoon, 1923, more than four years after the signing of the Armistice the people of the great Republic of the West, a government conceived in liberty and dedicated to the proposition that all men are created equal, are still discussing the question of whether or not they should release their political prisoners. I cannot regard such a fact as other than strange and to my mind intolerable. Let us hasten to make our belief as a people known that the time has come when we should without further delay give these men their freedom. (Applause.)

I do not know, and of course therefore I am not permitted to conjecture, just why the government at Washington has hesitated to grant amnesty to these political prisoners. But I believe nevertheless that good can only come from a thorough discussion of these matters in public—I believe furthermore that public opinion always has a wholesome effect upon such questions as these. It at least, properly expressed, aids the Executive department in coming to a conclusion upon this proposition. After all, we are occasionally a government of the people. (Laughter and Applause.) There is one power which we all down at Washington respect, and that is, the power of public opinion. I have no doubt at all that if the American people were thoroughly informed as to the facts there would be an undoubted public opinion upon this question, and I have no doubt either that a very large majority of the American people would favor the immediate release of these men.

Let us bear in mind, my friends, that these men are not in prison at the present time by reason of any acts of violence to either person or property. Whatever might have inhered in the case with reference to these matters in the beginning has long since passed out of the case and these men are in prison today, separated from their families, deprived of an opportunity of earning a livlihood, their health being undermined for the sole and only reason that they expressed their opinions concerning the war and the activities of the government in the prosecution of the war. They are distinctly and unquestionably political prisoners in the true sense of that term. They are not there for the violation of ordinary criminal statutes or for deeds of violence of any kind.

Let us not be misled into the belief that they are there because of a conviction of crimes of that nature. These things were cleared away either by the decisions of the court or by virtue of the expiration of any punishment which may have been assessed and they are there today solely for either writing or speaking concerning the war or the prosecution of the war or some matter relating to the war.

They are, in other words in prison some four years after the war for expressing an opinion in regard to it. I was thinking today as I was reflecting over this situation that six months before the time we declared war some of the most prominent members of the government at that time would have been guilty of the same offense for which these men are now in prison. (Applause.) Six months before we entered the war it was considered most objectionable in the United States to advocate going into the war. Six months before the war began we were told that this great world war had its roots in causes which we did not understand and with which we were not concerned and that we should keep out of it. It would seem that the gravest offense upon the part of these men, so far as expressing their views was concerned, is that they were late in catching up with the procession. They did not or were unable, to adjust their views to the changed condition of affairs as readily as others.

Do not misunderstand me. I am one of those who believe that when my country is at war, engaged in deadly strife with an enemy, as a matter of policy we ought to surrender our individual views and get behind the government if we can possibly do so. In such times we ought to reconcile ourselves to our government's successful conduct of the war. But while that is my belief, it is also my contention, grounded in the deepest principles of free government, that if a man thinks a war is unjust or improvident, or that it is being carried on in a corrupt manner it is his absolute right to say so. (Applause.) Indeed, if it is a question of the method of carrying on the war and he believes it is unwise or unjust it is his duty to say so.

Let me call your attention to the views of a most distinguished American lawyer now a United States Senator, with reference to the nature of these cases and the evidence upon which the convictions rest. Honorable George Wharton Pepper has long been a leader, if not the leader, of the Philadelphia bar. He is not a gentleman who is calculated to permit his sympathies to control his judgment with reference to questions of law or procedure in courts. He has imposed upon himself the very noble service as an American lawyer, believing it to be a part of the duty of an American lawyer, the investigation of these cases. He has performed the high service of going through the records of at least one of the trials and has passed his opinion upon the nature of the case. May I read a single paragraph from his statement. He says: "I satisfied myself that in not one of the twenty-eight cases I had looked into did the evidence justify a continuance of restraint."

Not one of the twenty-eight cases which he had examined disclosed sufficient evidence, in the first place, to justify a conviction of these men for this particular offense. In other words, my friends, they were convicted under the compelling influence of passion and the excitement and fears which accompany war. It is a fearful thing to have men lie in prison when there is not sufficient evidence, according to great and dispassionate lawyers, to warrant their incarceration. It is a fearful indictment against the justice and proceedings of government. Add to that, my friends, to the insufficiency of the evidence, the fact that they are now there solely and alone for expressing their political opinions, and it becomes almost incredible that they should longer remain in prison.

We are Americans. We believe that our government can do justice to our people. If by reason of the excitement of war we err at a particular hour in our history, in the name of our government and in the name of the liberty we love, let us correct it as soon as we can after the passions of war shall have passed. It is human to err but it is inhuman to refuse to correct an error after we are thoroughly cognizant of it.

Senator Pepper further says: "Each of these men presented a problem in human liberty. I am hopeful that the President will act, hopeful that the public generally will understand that none of these is a case of violence or injury to life or property. None is a case in which there was any conspiracy to hinder the United States. And the most there is against these men are their utterances in and out of print expressing opposition to the war, or indifference to it." And for these expressions the sentences ran as high as twenty-six years.

A VOICE. That's a shame.

SENATOR BORAH. Yes, it seems a shame. (Applause.)

I am now going to read a paragraph from the report of an officer of the Army who was assigned to examine the evidence in some of these cases. I speak with all respect of an officer of the regular army, but will say,—and he would be proud, I presume, to have me say,— that his training and the training of all such officers is such as to lead them to look with great scrutiny and with rigid criticism on anything which partakes of the nature of opposition to the government engaged in war. Certainly, such an officer would not consciously be biased in favor of one who was guilty of interfering with the government under such circumstances. Major Lanier says, after going through the record: "I do not think if I had been on the jury I would have convicted a single one of these men." And remember he had been assigned the particular task as a representative of the government to investigate the record and to report. "Because in my judgment there was not sufficient evidence presented to prove that these men were guilty of the conspiracy with which they were charged." Again he says: "I am of the opinion that these men were convicted contrary to the law and the evidence solely because they were leaders in an organization against which opinion was incensed and the verdict rendered was due to public hysteria of the time."

Some might say that, owing to my views upon certain questions, I might be unnecessarily, illogically in sympathy with these men. I am not in sympathy with any man who wilfully commits crime. I read these two statements, however, one from a distinguished lawyer, another from an officer of the army whose business it has been to examine the record, as conclusive proof of the fact that these men are in prison, not only for expressing their views, but they are in prison without sufficient evidence to justify them being there, regardless of the crime with which they have been charged. (Applause.)

What therefore is the real, the controlling,

reason for denying these political prisoners their freedom. It is not, in my opinion, the offense for which they were convicted. It is not because the court record condemns them. It is for another offense—unknown to the criminal code and undisclosed in the sentences under which they are now serving. These men it is claimed are members of an organization known as the Industrial Workers of the World —an organization, as many of us believe, antagonistic in its teachings to the good order and happiness of society and to the principles of representative government. I understand they are members of this organization, some of them at least. Let that fact be conceded. Let it be conceded that they are believers in these insupportable doctrines. But these men are not now in prison, under sanction of law, for sabotage, for acts of violence to either persons or property. They are being punished for political offenses—charged with having offered opinions and views upon the war and the activities of the government in the prosecution of the war. If these men have violated any law touching the character of the organization of which they are members, if they have been guilty of acts of violence defined by any provision of the criminal code, for these offenses let them be charged, and if convicted, be punished, in accordance with the established laws and procedure of a government of law. If they have come under the ban of our immigration laws, let them be dealt with in the manner there prescribed. But it is manifestly unjust, it is an act of tyranny, to put men in prison because of political opinions and keep them there because they are members of an unpopular organization. It is the very essence of despotism to punish men for offense for which they have not been convicted. It is the first essential of justice in a government of law to punish men only and alone for offenses defined by law. It is the dominating tenet of tyranny to punish men for what they think—for what they believe. It is a cardinal rule under free institutions to punish men only and alone for what they do. These men are not only now suffering for offenses of which they have not been convicted but for things of which the criminal law has not yet taken notice. Such procedure, such treatment of our citizens, be they high or low, wise or unwise, correct in their views or wholly erroneous, brings government into disparagement, if not contempt. Such procedure is a prostitution of our courts

—a perversion of the first principles of constitutional government.

But there is a much broader principle, my friends, involved in this matter, one of far deeper concern than the freedom of fifty-three men. That is important, supremely, important, to these individuals and their families. Indeed, it is important to all who love justice. No one can do other than sympathize with them in their present condition and yet I say that there is a much deeper and wider principle involved, one touching more closely the interests of the people of the United States. In my opinion, at the bottom of the controversy there lies the question of what constitutes free speech and free press under the American flag. (Prolonged applause.) May I trespass upon your time long enough to read from an ancient document known as the Constitution of the United States. (Laughter and applause.) I read a single paragraph. It is so simple and so plain that a man need not be a lawyer in order to understand it. In fact, it sometimes seems that the less law one knows, the better he understands the Constitution. (Applause.) But it is this particular clause in the Constitution which interests me so far as this situation is concerned. It says: "Congress shall make no

law respecting an establishment of religion"
—make no law—"or prohibit the free exercise
thereof or abridging the freedom of speech."
Not deny the freedom of speech, not prohibit
the freedom of speech, but not ever shall the
Congress abridge the freedom of speech. There
are many in this country who delight in writing history and who are always telling us that
the Fathers, after all, were a very conservative,
reactionary group of men, (Laughter), that
while they professed to build a free government they built a Republic so rigid that it does
not give sufficient action or freedom of action
to the citizen.

I read only a short time ago a book by a
distinguished educator in this country who undertook to convince his readers that the Fathers were not believers in free government at
all. Well, I wish we believed in free government and in the great principles of free speech
and free press just as thoroughly as they did.
(Applause.) When you consider that this
Constitution was written in 1787, adopted finally in 1789, at a time when every government
in the world looked upon this effort to establish a free government as a mere experiment,
as a dream which would pass in a few months,
when you realize the circumstances and envi-

ronments under which this government was formed, you can easily understand what the faith of the Fathers must have been who had the courage to write into the fundamental law "that Congress should pass no law abridging the freedom of speech." Yet even in these days we hear people say that those who framed the Constitution had no faith in the people. (Applause.) Abridge the freedom of speech or the press? Certainly the press. (Laughter.) I am just as much in favor of a free press as I am of free speech—they go together. And the right of the people peaceably to assemble and to petition their government for redress of grievances goes along with free speech and free press. Without these things there can be no such thing as a free people. A great American has well said: "You can chain up all other human rights, but leave speech free and it will unchain all the rest."

It was my opinion, as I have stated, at the time of the passage of the Espionage law that it violated the first amendment of the Constitution of the United States. But we passed it. The Supreme Court has held that it did not violate the provision of the Constitution. And while we are bound by that decision so long as it stands and while I have great and profound respect for the Supreme Court of the United States, it has not changed by opinion in regard to the constitutionality of this law.

We ought not to be afraid of the freedom of speech so long as it relates to the discussion of the activities of the government and to the discussion of public questions. No man has a right to advise the commission of crime. No man has a right to insist upon the violation of law. But every American citizen under our Constitution has the right to discuss with the greatest of freedom all questions relating to political matters or as to the wisdom of any course which the government may be pursuing.

It is incredible to me that in a particular exigency men should be prohibited from earnestly expressing their views as to the wisdom or unwisdom of an act or a policy upon the part of the government. (Applause.) I thank God every time I think of it that no Espionage law, no repression of free speech, availed or prevailed at the time that the Elder Pitt and Edmund Burke were denouncing the war of the English government against the American colonies. We were then fighting for our freedom and these brave men denounced in language as immortal as freedom itself the war of the English government upon the American colonies. (Applause.)

But there is a peculiar doctrine which has come to have recognition in this country to which I must refer. It was said during the late war that as soon as war was declared the Constitution of the United States was in a sense suspended, that the Congress could pass any law it saw fit to pass. At first, that seemed to me to be a subject of amusement, and I still really think it is. But as a matter of fact, it was seriously advocated by learned and able men, legislators and executive departments. It was upon that theory and apparently upon that principle that many things were done during the war. For myself, I want to repudiate it once and for all. I trust that no such vicious and un-American doctrine will ever be seriously considered by the people of this country. There is only one way that you can change the Constitution of the United States or suspend any of its provisions, and that is, in the same way and by the same power that made it, to wit, the people of the United States themselves in the manner pointed out by the Constitution. (Applause.) Every clause, every line, every paragraph, of that Great Charter obtains in time of war just the same as in time of peace.

(Applause.)   Washington was something of
a soldier.   Hamilton understood something of
war.   The framers of the Constitution had all
passed through a great conflict of eight years
in length.   They undoubtedly understood that
the Republic would in all probability be called
upon to wage war in the future.   Do you suppose they thought they were building a government or writing a Constitution which was
to obtain during peaceful days only?   They
wrote a Constitution sufficient and efficient
to carry on the work of peace and also to carry
on war.   The Constitution gives sufficient
power by its own terms for the conduct of
war and none of its provisions are suspended,
or annuled by the declaration of war.   Any
other theory would be perfectly vicious.   It
would be to write it into our very government
the doctrine of the tyrants that necessity
knows no law.

I pause here to read in support of this proposition a paragraph from a celebrated decision
of the Supreme Court of the United States.
Let those who think that our Constitution was
made for peace and not for war turn to this
decision and read it in full.   The Court says:
"The Constitution of the United States is a law
for rulers and people, equally in war and in

peace, and covers with the shield of its protection all classes of men at all times and under all circumstances. No doctrine involving more pernicious consequences was ever invented by the wit of man than that any of its provisions can be suspended during any of the great exigencies of government. Such a doctrine leads directly to anarchy or despotism, but the theory of necessity on which it is based is false; for the government within the Constitution has all the powers granted to it which are necessary to preserve its existence as has been happily proved by the result of the great effort to overthrow its just authority."

There, my friends, coming from the Supreme Court, is the true doctrine. The Constitution obtains in time of war as well as in time of peace. The first amendment of the Constitution can be construed no differently in time of war than in time of peace. An Espionage law that is unconstitutional in time of peace is unconstitutional in time of war. Let us have faith in our government and also faith in our people.

This is, therefore, not a mere question today of the liberation of fifty-three men, important as that is. It involves the great underlying principle of free government. And our Pres-

ident, who is now in the South seeking the
rest to which he is entitled and the rest which
I sincerely hope may come to him, could do no
greater service to the cause of American institutions than to turn aside for a moment and
reannounce our devotion to these plain provisions of the Constitution of the United States,
provisions of the Constitution which have been
construed and about which there is no doubt
as to their meaning.

But let us turn over a page of history and
take a lesson from the past, from men of great
prestige and still holding the affections of the
American people. Let me read you a line from
the speech of a truly beloved American.

You will recall that Abraham Lincoln did
not agree with the policy on the Mexican war.
In a debate in the House of Representatives
he said; speaking of the President of the United States: "He knows not where he is. He is
bewildered, confounded and miserably per-
plexed man. God grant he may be able to
show that there is not something about his
conscience more painful than his mental per-
plexity." That was said in the midst of the
war. He thought the war was unjust and unwise and he said so. He thought it was being
carried on from wrong motives and he said so.

He believed it was against conscience and he so declared. If the late Espionage law had been upon the statute books and someone had seen fit to invoke it, he doubtless would have been sent to the penitentiary instead of being, to the everlasting honor of the American people, shortly thereafter made President. He had a perfect right to express himself. But he had no better right to express himself than the humblest member of an organization or the humblest citizen of the United States.

I read a paragraph from a speech of Daniel Webster, the great constitutional lawyer and distinguished statesman, who was also opposed to the Mexican war: "We are, in my opinion, in a most unnecessary and therefore a most unjustifiable war. I hope we are nearing the close of it. I attend carefully and anxiously to every rumor and every breeze that brings to us any report that the effusion of blood caused in my judgment by a rash and unjustifiable proceeding on the part of the government may cease. Now, sir, the law of nations instructs us that there are wars of pretext. The history of the world proves that there have been and we are not now without proof that there are wars waged on pretext, that is on pretenses, where the cause assigned is not the true cause. That I believe on my conscience is the true character of a war now being waged against Mexico. I believe it to be a war of pretexts, a war in which the true motive is not distinctly avowed but in which pretenses, afterthoughts, evasions, and other methods are employed to put a case before the community which is not the true case." Men may differ, some may think that Webster was in error as to judgment and some may think he was right. But there are thousands and hundreds of thousands who believe that the Mexican war was not justified. But do you think it ever occurred to Mr. Lincoln or to Mr. Webster that, believing the war was without justification, unwise and unrighteous, they did not have the right as American citizens to say so. What I am pleading for today is not a new rule, not a new precedent, but an old rule and the maintenance of an old precedent, a rule in which our Fathers believed, which our forbears would never have given up and a rule which is written in the Constitution of the United States and which the great statesmen of America have defended from that time until this. (Applause.)

Let me say a few words about another phase of this question. There is still another reason why I feel so keenly about this matter. I think this is one of the steps which should be taken to help break this fearful psychology of war which still remains with us, notwithstanding four years have passed since the signing of the Armistice. You will all remember the morning after the signing of the Armistice,—what a happy world it seemed at that time. You could not meet anyone that happiness was not written on his or her very countenance. We thought we were passing out of the bitterness, away from the hatreds and the passions, which had cursed the world for many, many months. We felt that we were about to escape from that fearful condition of mind which had been expressing itself in so many ugly ways, hoping to get rid of the antipathies, the hatreds, and the vengeance which naturally come with war. We felt that we were turning our backs upon these things and would again be free from them. But while the fighting had ceased upon the battlefield and the armies had surrendered, we know today, as a matter of fact, that we did not get away from the passions which came with the war.

Look over Europe today, torn and distracted from corner to corner, and side to side, by the same racial antipathies, the same hatreds, the

same turmoil, the same strife, the same urge
for blood. Where, my friends, is this all going to end? Shall we not make a brave fight to
get away from these things. You may talk
your leagues and your alliances, your schemes
for peace, but if you cannot get rid of this passion, this bitterness, this urge for blood, there
can be no peace, (applause) there can be no
peace until we turn our backs upon the ugly
things which came with the war. Let us take
one step, at least, release the political prisoners and put that ugly record behind us.

It is a little thing in one sense, an inconse-
quential thing, to turn loose fifty-three men,
fifty-three out of 110,000,000 people, but it is
an awful thing on the other hand to keep them
in prison, an awful thing for the United States
to say that even one man shall be restrained in
prison four years after the war for expressing
his views as to the wisdom of the war. If we
can do that my friends, if America can get rid
of these things, if we can put behind us these
questions which have torn and distracted us
for years, then shall we again become a happy
and contented peoples. That is Americanism.
Americanism is liberty. And what is liberty?
It is not a mere right to be free from chains,
it is not a mere right to be outside the prison

walls—liberty is also the right to express your-
self, to entertain your views, to defend your
policies, to treat yourself and your neighbors
as free and independent agents under a great
representative Republic. (Applause.)

What we ask today, what we ask of our
President and the government at Washington,
therefore, is not to depart from old precedents
or to establish new precedents, but to go back,
to return to those principles upon which the
Fathers built and without which this government cannot exist. Free speech is the supreme
test of free institutions.

Do not let us mislead ourselves into the belief that the principles which we discuss here
today or the question which we discuss concern alone these men who are in prison. It is a
far more vital question than that. There is no
subject, there can be no subject, of deeper concern in these days than that of preserving these
civil rights of the citizen. It is a matter which
relates directly and immediately to the welfare, the security and the happiness of all. But
it is especially of the highest concern to the
average citizen. Those of influence and uncommon ability, of commanding wealth, may
secure rights under any condition or under any
kind of government sufficient to make life com-

fortable, or at least endurable. But the average man or woman, the man of limited means, or circumscribed influence, finds security only and alone in the great Charter itself—a Charter binding alike upon the courts and the Congress, upon majorities and minorities, and upon the rich and the poor. Newspapers of great prestige, I observe, always publish, whatever the occasion, whatever they please to publish. Men of great power will, as they did during the war, say whatever they choose to say. It is the less influential or the less feared politically, it is the less powerful, who lie in jails or purchase their freedom by becoming the intellectual slaves of those temporarily in control. The Constitution however in its guarantees makes no distinctions, it knows no class, it recognizes neither prestige nor poverty—under its terms all stand upon a plane of equality. All therefore who prize human liberty will be jealous to see the Constitution administered according to its letter and its spirit. That is the price of free government.

The framers of the Constitution were the most practical of men. They were not intellectual adventurers. They were not dreamers. They knew the worth of that concrete thing called liberty and they knew how to secure it.

There was really nothing new in the bill of rights. They were rights and privileges which the hard experience of centuries had wrought out and laid at their doors. For these rights and privileges men had gone to prison and even to death. The rust of human blood had made sacred the very things with which some are now disposed to trifle. But the Fathers, knowing the value of these rights, incorporated them safely in the fundamental law. They knew you would have to protect the citizen against majorities just as in ancient days he was to be protected against kings and despots. They gathered up the experiences, those bitter experiences, which had cut away the superfluous and the false and incorporated them in a place where they ought never to be challenged nor disregarded. They had the courage and the practical common sense to put those things where they believed they could never be forfeited, save by the people themselves. But now we find, sirs, that they are being forfeited by those whose highest duty it is to preserve them—those who have been entrusted with power.

The assaults these days upon the Constitution, and particularly upon the Bill of Rights, are persistent and insidious, as tireless as they are dishonorable. They are made under specious pleas and for all kinds of purpose and with all kinds of proclaimed good intentions. The most pronounced and precious privileges of the citizens they dare not openly challenge, but under the cover of public service they are nevertheless frittered away. But however made, or by whomsoever or for whatsoever purpose, men who really believe in a representative Republic, will resist these aggressions whenever and however and by whomsoever made. We cannot afford to barter these rights or sacrifice them for any cause or for any purpose or under any circumstances. It may sometimes seem advisable to do so for a day or to meet some particular emergency, but in the end it will prove a costly experiment. Whether in peace or in war, they should be guarded, religiously guarded. The people may change the Constitution if they choose. They may rehabilitate these rights from time to time in the manner pointed out by the Constitution. But so long as the Constitution remains as it is, it is the sacred duty, as well as the high privilege of those who stand in places of responsibility, to see that it is preserved in all its integrity.

XXI

PROPOSAL FOR AN INTERNATIONAL ECONOMIC CONFERENCE
January 30, 1923

(The following October 26, 1923, Secretary Hughes announced his willingness to consider an economic conference under certain conditions.)

Resolved, That the President is authorized and requested to invite such governments as he may deem necessary or expedient to send representatives to a conference which shall be charged with the duty of considering the economic problems now obtaining throughout the world with a view of arriving at such adjustments, or settlement, as may seem essential to the restoration of trade and to the establishment of sound financial and business conditions; and also to consider the subject of further limitation of armaments with a view of reaching an understanding or agreement upon said matter both by land and by sea, and particularly relative to limiting the construction of all types and sizes of subsurface and surface craft of ten thousand tons standard displacement, or less, and of aircraft.

XXII

SHALL THE CONSTITUTION OF THE UNITED STATES BE NULLIFIED?

(Address before the Citizens Conference on Law Enforcement, Washington, D. C., October 15, 1923.)

Mr. Chairman, Ladies and Gentlemen:

As this is the end of a three days' session for you and late in the afternoon, I shall bear in mind that I must be brief. The subject which has been assigned to me is "Shall the Constitution of the United States be Nullified?" This brings before us the Constitution as an entirety, as a charter of government. It includes every part of the Great Charter. It covers the whole document, a document which has been our pride, our bond of union, and the basis of our power, and which is a guarantee of our future. The supreme question which is presented is whether we have consciously, or unconsciously, come to the conclusion that we can no longer abide by a written constitution or that we may disregard the principles under which the government was organized. There is no theme in which I could feel a deeper interest and yet none which I could feel less capable of adequately presenting. It is a much greater question than any possible question which could arise by reason of any particular provision of the Constitution. It involves the supreme proposition of whether we are a people who believe in law and order. While this or that individual may be interested in this or that particular provision of the Constitution, we must bear in mind, however, that only as we observe the great Charter as a whole and live up to it in its integrity and express by word and action our belief in constitutional government, shall we make headway in preserving the integrity of any particular provision.

The subject which has been assigned to me does not devolve upon me the duty of arguing the wisdom or unwisdom of any provision of the Constitution. That question was settled when any particular provision was placed in the Constitution. I take the instrument as I find it—the crystalized views of a nation and mean to insist that it shall be maintained and enforced as written. No one can question, no one desires to question, I assume, the right of a citizen, or a body of citizens, to urge a change in the Constitution, to take out any provision which they deem unwise, or to put in any additional provision which they may think proper. No one can challenge the citizenship of those who, candidly and openly, advocate a modification of the Great Charter. The supreme test of a free government is the right of a people to write and unwrite its constitution and its laws. The supreme test of good citizenship is to obey the laws when written. If we are not prepared to obey the laws when written, consciously or unconsciously, we have put aside the only principle upon which a representative republic can exist.

In discussing the integrity of the Constitution, I want to go back in history a short way. I think in a large measure the disregard which obtains for the Constitution is one which has grown up by reason of most unfortunate precedents. It seems to me our duty to review these precedents and to bring home to ourselves the question of whether we may not do something in the way of removing some of the precedents which have been established. It was often said during the late war that as soon as war was declared the Constitution of the United States was in a sense, or in some respects, suspended and that the Congress could pass any law it should see fit to pass. This is

a strange doctrine. When it was first announced, it seemed to me almost absurd, and
yet it was seriously advocated by learned and
able men, accepted by legislators and executive
departments. The view was honestly entertained by people whose integrity of purpose
you could not question. But a more vicious
principle could not be announced under a written constitution. For myself, I repudiate it
once and for all. No such dangerous and un-
American doctrine should be accepted or admitted by the people of this country. The
Constitution of the United States cannot be
changed, modified or amended or suspended,
or any part of it, except in the manner and
through the processes pointed out by the Constitution itself, that is, by the people of the
United States. (Applause.) Every clause,
every line, every paragraph of that Great Charter obtains in time of war the same as in time
of peace. I am not going to discuss this proposition at length. But think a moment of the
contention that because the Congress of the
United States sees fit to declare war, they
would be able to suspend or modify the provisions of the Constitution under which we
live. The supreme dictators of ancient days

would not have asked for any different doctrine.

I pause long enough to read to you a single paragraph upon that subject from a noted and noble decision of the Supreme Court of the United States. It contains all I need say upon this subject: "The Constitution of the United States is a law for rulers and people, equally in war and in peace, and covers with the shield of its protection all classes of men at all times and under all circumstances. No doctrine involving more pernicious consequences was ever invented by the wit of man than that any of its provisions can be suspended during any of the great exigencies of government. Such a doctrine leads directly to anarchy or despotism, but the theory of necessity on which it is based is false; for the government within the Constitution has all the powers granted to it which are necessary to preserve its existence as has been happily proved by the result of the great effort to overthrow its just authority." That, my friends, is the true doctrine and the only one which we, as a free people, can afford to accept—that the Constitution binds every individual, every citizen, every organization and all departments of government; that it binds the Supreme Court of the United States and the Congress and every officer of the executive department, the same in time of war as in time of peace; and let the people of the United States maintain this at all times. Let the people of the United States understand that this is their instrument of government and that with the people, and the people alone, rests the power to change it, and so understanding and so believing they will have infinitely more respect for it in the future than if they should come to the belief that it is within the power of the Congress of the United States to change, modify or suspend it.

Let's follow this matter a little farther, and observe some of the consequences of this doctrine, that war suspends the Constitution,—consequences which may not be passed over. I have often thought if I were going to be asked to select any particular provision of the Constitution, or any particular amendment of the Constitution, which I should regard as more sacred than all others, it would be the First Amendment, guaranteeing free speech, a free press, and the right of peaceable assemblage. Around this great principle the whole cause of free government has been successfully organized and fought. A great American has truly declared that you may chain up all human rights save the right of free speech, but leave speech free and it will unchain all the rest. The principle of the First Amendment of the Constitution is absolutely essential to the organization and maintenance of any form of free government. Indeed, it is the supreme test of a free government. I beg leave therefore to refer to it for a moment. May I read it to you? "Congress shall make no law respecting an establishment of religion, or prohibit the free exercise thereof, or abridging the freedom of speech or of the press, or the right of the people peaceably to assemble and to petition the government for a redress of grievances." That is the First Amendment, and if there is a principle in that Constitution that is sacred, there it is written. And while I may subject myself to criticism, in my opinion, that provision of the Constitution has been disregarded and violated for six long years. (Applause.) Such are the effects of war upon the Constitution; such are the effects of war in breeding hate and intolerance; that there are men in prison today—not for the destruction of property, not for acts of violence, but because they were charged with expressing their political views upon political questions. But what is still more startling, they are there without any legal evidence sufficient to hold them. (Applause.) I have here upon my desk, but which I shall not take time to read, ample evidence of what I say to you. I would count myself a whining hypocrite if I should come here to ask for the enforcement of the Eighteenth Amendment and dared not open my lips in behalf of the men who have been denied the protection of the First Amendment of the Constitution. (Applause.) If I cannot speak for the Constitution as a whole, I should not speak at all. And if I do not respect the Constitution as a whole, I am unfit to speak in behalf of any part of it.

Let us announce to the people that all the provisions of this Constitution are sacred to us, that we propose to uphold and maintain them and devoutly respect them. Let it be understood that we are here asking for the enforcement and the maintenance of the Great Charter under which we live in all its fullness and in all its integrity. Let's go to the people with a proposition that it is a question of order and law—a question of orderly and regulated liberty—for which we are contending; and we shall make progress with reference to those things in which we are peculiarly interested at this time.

My friends, there are other provisions which I should like to mention and which I think are not receiving proper consideration. But I have referred to these particular provisions to illustrate to you my belief that when you come to defend the Constitution, you must look at it as it is, as the greatest instrument of government ever devised by the wit of man, and that it is that instrument of government, the integrity of which is so essential to our happiness, our liberty, and our future prestige and power, for which we are contending. I recognize, of course, that the storm center of the Constitution just now is the Eighteenth Amendment. Let us discuss that for a short time.

Perhaps no provision of the Constitution ever went into that instrument after more consideration and more deliberation, more agitation, more discussion, than the Eighteenth Amendment. Thirty-three states prior to its adoption had established statewide prohibition; the subject had been discussed among and before the people for the last fifty years; every State legislature had adopted the principle in some form or other. Finally, the amendment came before Congress, was discussed in both bodies of Congress, went to the respective legislatures of the States, was considered by the legislatures, and ratified by all the States except two. Certainly, no one can contend that this provision of the Constitution is there by accident. Certainly, they cannot successfully contend that it went there without proper discussion and consideration. The amendment is there as the deliberate, expressed will and wish and purpose of the American people. It carries the same sanctity and the same force as any other provision of the Constitution. It is there, and so long as it remains there, it is vital to the cause of good government, to the cause of constitutional government, and to the cause of law and order, that it be lived up to and maintained in all its integrity. There can be no more vital problem presented to a free people than the problem of whether or not they can hold and maintain the Constitution of which they have deliberately written.

What did this constitutional amendment do and propose to do? It established, in the first place, a great national policy. It didn't undertake to deal with the liquor question as an article of interstate commerce, or as a matter exclusively for Federal control; but the Eighteenth Amendment declared a great national policy, to-wit, that intoxicating liquors should not be manufactured, sold or transported throughout the United States, or any part of it, that they should neither be imported nor exported. Here, therefore, was a national policy declared and written into the fundamental law as the deliberate, the unmistakably, expressed will and wish of the people of the United States. The question presented therefore is a greater question than that of prohibition. Important as the question of prohibition is, the question which is now presented is the enforcement of the amendment, the higher and bigger and broader question of whether we, as a free people, can maintain and enforce the provisions of the Constitution as they have been written. That involves, as my friend here has said, the whole question of constitutional integrity, of constitutional morality—indeed of the ultimate success of free government itself. Let us view it from that standpoint as we consider the question.

But the constitutional provision went farther than the mere declaration of a national policy. It declared, or granted, the power to both the State and National government to execute and make effective that national policy. It gave concurrent power to the state and to the

national government to see that this policy
was made effective. It did not leave it to the
national government. It did not withdraw
from the States the powers which they had had
and lodge them in the national government;
but after declaring a national policy, it placed
the obligation upon both the State and the
National government alike to enforce it.

There has been much discussion about the
duty of the State under these circumstances.
It is a subject about which earnest and able
men may differ. But the discussion has
seemed to me to proceed upon too narrow
and too technical a basis. It is not alone
a question of what the State is legally
bound to do or what it may be compelled
to do, but what should the State as an
integral part of the American Union and
acting in the integrity and purposes of that
Union do. Certainly we cannot mandamus a
State to pass a law or to execute or enforce a
law. But there is an infinitely more compelling power calling the State into action, and
that is, the fact that the State is an integral
part of the American Union. The whole purpose, the very existence of the Union requires
and depends upon concerted action in carrying out the aims and purposes of the Union

as expressed in the Federal Constitution. We live under two sovereignties. We seek to combine and utilize local and national interests in one grand purpose. We are endeavoring in this way to work out the great problem of representative government. Is not every State a part, and anxious to be considered a part, of that purpose? Is not every State interested and deeply concerned in working out that problem? Is not every State bound in the most solemn way to contribute to the fullest extent of its ability to the solution of that problem? Who wants to be considered a slacker in the most sublime task ever undertaken in the affairs of government—that of demonstrating that a people may govern themselves, govern under established law and in the spirit of regulated liberty? Does anyone think such a task possible of achievement, if sovereign States withdraw or withhold their most zealous support of the supreme law of the land or any part of it? Forget for a moment that the Eighteenth Amendment covers the question of prohibition and think of it only as a part of the Charter under which we live and to which we owe allegiance and support, and how plainly the duty of every individual and of every State appears.

I know it is argued that the State's sovereignty has been encroached upon unjustly by this provision of the Constitution. But I contend most earnestly that goes only to the question of change in the Constitution, a right which no one can deny to those who would undertake it. But it is wholly irrelevant upon the question of maintaining the Constitution as it is written. It is not for prohibition as such that I am speaking this evening, but for the integrity of the Constitution, the more fundamental and indispensable and vital principle of government, the maintenance of law. If the proposition of change in the Constitution were up for discussion, the wisdom or unwisdom of doing so would be a wholly different matter from that which we are now considering. But prohibitionist, or anti-prohibitionist, we ought as good loyal citizens to be willing to support the law so long as it is the law. There are other amendments to the Constitution which thousands of our people dislike. But they are there. They are the expressed will and purpose of the whole nation. They should be lived up to and enforced. One State may be dissatisfied with the Fifteenth Amendment, another state may be dissatisfied with the Fourteenth Amendment, another state may be dissatisfied with the Thirteenth Amendment, another may be dissatisfied with this or that portion of the Constitution. Suppose the doctrine which has been invoked that a State may stand aside and withdraw its support were applied by all the different states of the Union as expressed by their people as to some particular provision of the Constitution, as Daniel Webster said many years ago, our entire structure would go to pieces. If someone thinks the Eighteenth Amendment is unwise and desires to come out before the American people and advocate its being taken out of the Constitution, neither you nor I can criticize him, that is a right which he has. But so long as it is there written; so long as it is a part of it; the question of state rights can have no hearing when the question of enforcement is up for consideration. (Applause.) The question of State rights was fought out when it was before the State legislatures; and the States, as sovereignties, said: We delegate this power and are willing to cooperate with the national government. And it is not the part of any government or any individual representing a state after that judgment has been rendered to say: In my opinion, it encroaches upon State rights.

(Applause.) It is a fearful doctrine which has been preached to us, this doctrine of disregarding the Constitution under the claim of state rights. It feeds lawlessness like the poison of the swamp gives the germs of disease. It is a libel on the whole theory of the American Union. It is an indictment of the whole superb scheme of 1789.

There is a well-organized movement in this country against a class of people who it is said are unfriendly to our form of government and our Constitution, a class of people who are designated as reds and radicals. Those who are uneasy about the rights of property as guaranteed by the Constitution are greatly interested in this work. They have a thorough organization dealing with the subjects of anarchy, communism and bolshevism, and those things which they feel undermine our government and destroy the stability of our institutions. I thoroughly sympathize with their desires to inculcate respect for and loyalty to our institutions. I think you cannot spend too much time in educating the American people in the worth of the institutions under which we live and of the value of our form of government. I agree with the encomiums which you constantly find in our literature dealing with this class of people. I think these people, so long as they go about it in a moderate and educational way, are doing a good service by constantly calling attention to the inestimable worth of our fundamental law and what its defiance or destruction means. A man who comes to our shores and openly defies our Constitution is a most unworthy creature. But he is not so reprehensible, so much to be criticized, it seems to me, as the man who has been reared in this country, who has had an opportunity to know the beneficent worth of our institutions, who has witnessed the value through all these years of the law under which our government lives and who still disregards or defies some particular provision or amendment because it runs counter to his personal interests or personal views or personal vices. Let me say here today,—not all of them, of course,—but many of those people of property, many of those who are much agitated over the question of foreign propaganda and its undermining effect upon our Constitution, are the most pronounced, insistent, and persistent, violators of the Eighteenth Amendment to the Constitution. (Applause). The hot bed, the scouting, noisy rendezvous of lawlessness, of cynical defiance to the Eighteenth Amend-

ment, are among those of social standing, of
large property interests, and in the wealthier
homes. (Applause.) Without their patron-
age, their protection, and their example, the
bootlegger could easily be brought within the
control of the law. (Applause). I repeat
again, I am thoroughly in sympathy with their
anxiety over foreign influence upon the Constitution, but I must say in all sincerity that just
to the extent that they undermine respect for
the Constitution, respect for law, by the lives
which they lead and the examples which they
set and by the influence which they exert
against the Eighteenth Amendment, just in
that proportion, to that extent, they are also
undermining those provisions of the Constitution which protect property. (Applause.) The
Eighteenth Amendment is in the Constitution
by the same authority as the Fifth Amendment which throws its protection around life
and property. The undermining of one undermines the other. The Eighteenth Amendment
is in the Constitution by the same authority
and with the same sanctity as the Fourteenth
Amendment which stands between the State
and the property holder against all assaults
by the State. That which undermines the
Eighteenth Amendment undermines the Four-

teenth Amendment. The red sits in his darkly lighted room around his poorly laden table and denounces those provisions of the Constitution placed there to protect property. The white sits in his brilliantly lighted room about his richly laden table and defies or denounces the provisions of the Constitution placed there in the belief they would protect the home. I leave it to all good citizens whether it is not true that both are traveling the road of lawlessness, both sowing the seeds of destruction, both undermining the whole fabric of law and order.

Let these people of influence who insist upon satisfying their appetites against the expressed will of the American people understand that they cannot have their property secure, that they cannot have their homes safe, that they cannot protect their wealth and those things which they deeply cherish, if they continue by their examples and by their precepts to sow the seeds of lawlessness throughout the United States. (Applause.)

We all know from a review of history that lawlessness is the insidious disease of republics. It is the one great malady against which every true patriot will ever be on guard. It is but a short step from the lawlessness of the man of means who scouts some part of the fundamental law because forsooth it runs counter to his wishes, to the soldier who may be called into the street to protect property, but, who taking counsel of his sympathies, fraternizes with the mob. The great question, therefore, before the American people now is, not that of prohibition, because that as a policy has been settled. The supreme question is: After we have determined as a people upon prohibition, whether we have the moral courage, the high determination, and the unwavering purpose to enforce that which we have written into the Constitution. (Applause.)

My friends, in these anxious days almost everyone has a plan or a scheme for the betterment of conditions—for the adjustment, or readjustment, of things which seem so strangely, so persistently, out of joint. But if I were going to inscribe a banner under which to make the fight for sound economics, for moral advancement, for a wise and efficient government, a banner with which to arouse the dispirited and discouraged millions of brave and loyal citizens, I would precede all other inscriptions, plans and pledges with that of obedience to the law because it is a law. (Ap-

plause.) There are hundreds and thousands
of people with the number daily increasing,
who would like to feel safe in their persons,
safe in their workshops and homes, who would
like to feel that justice can be administered
and laws enforced, and that the provisions of
our Constitution which protect property are
no more sacred than the provisions which protect human rights and moral values. (Applause.) What shall it profit that leaders
have planned and patriots have striven and
sacrificed through all these years if we have
come at last to the fearful, accursed, creed that
constitutions are to be disregarded, laws to be
evaded or defied, and finally, that we are to accept and put in practice the vicious and destructive and savage rule that every man is
a law unto himself. The bedrock, the granite,
formation upon which great civilizations and
powerful governments are built is obedience
to the law. That is the beginning and the end
of all good government. Without it we cannot hope for happiness and prosperity at home
or prestige and power abroad. We have arrived at the time when we can afford to, when
indeed we must, invoke the old virtues, appeal
again to the simple precepts of government,
and make obedience to law a cardinal tenet

of our political faith. (Applause.) We do not need a new faith. We need the simplicity, the directness, and the self-surrender of the old. We need to preach the creed of Washington, Jefferson, Jackson and Lincoln with a tongue of fire throughout the land. We need to have constitutional morality declared as was the gospel of old to the high and to the low, for against this neither "things present nor things to come shall prevail." (Applause.) You can no more leave behind the fundamental principles of right and justice, of respect for and obedience to law without paying the frightful penalty than a people, however high and strong in their material power, can abandon the simple pronouncements of Sinai without sinking into utter and hopeless degradation. (Applause.)

Sometime ago, Mr. Chairman, down in the great commonwealth of Kentucky I visited the place where Nancy Hanks, prematurely old and broken, nursed and nurtured and cared for the most extraordinary child yet born under the American flag. (Applause.) As you stoop and enter that hovel and reflect, as you will upon the squalor and the wretchedness which a century ago environed its improvident inmates, and then call up in memory the glory which came out of that hovel, the glory which has since filled the earth, you will feel a deeper reverence and a stronger love for these institutions of ours than you ever felt before. There will come to you and upon you a feeling which both humbles and makes you brave; a yearning to know what is to be the ultimate destiny of a "government of the people, by the people, and for the people." And when you lingeringly and reluctantly come to take your leave of this humble, this appealing place, enriched and inspired with the sensations and the fancies of the brief hour, and turn your face again toward the real world with its fearful unrest, its turbulent, distressful conditions, you will find yourself involuntarily saying: Give us again leaders of courage, men of vision, men who believe that right makes might, men with faith in the efficiency, the strength, the permanency, and the ultimate triumph of this blessed old Republic. (Applause.)